Praise for **FIANNA**

"At a time when too many scholarly   ... America offer only conventional pictures of victimization, parochialism, nostalgia, or political chicanery, *Fianna* breaks down such caricatures by providing an original story of Irish confidence, hope, and genuine historical influence. *Fianna* admirably fills a gaping void in the narrative of the Irish adventure in America."

— *Thomas Stanford, Ph. D., Christendom College, Front Royal, Virginia*

"*Fianna* puts a human face on the American Fenian (movement). Michael Plemmons engagingly portrays the tragicomic exploits of the Brotherhood by focusing on a little-known plan – little-known today, but very well known at the time – to invade and take over Canada. Plemmons' storytelling style is entertaining, and his history is even-handed, drawing on a wealth of primary source material."

— *Joel Stone, Curator, Detroit Historical Society*

"I thought I knew about the Fenians… but this was truly a revelation for me. It is 'history with an attitude.' Plemmons' observations and conclusions are consistently backed up by solid scholarship and credible evidence. I thoroughly enjoyed *Fianna*."

— *Stephen R. Williams, Director, Port Huron Museum, 1979-2006*

"Meticulously researched and deftly written, *Fianna* turns a spotlight on a little-known but critical period of Canadian history. Plemmons has unearthed surprising new details about the audacious and ill-fated 'Fenian rascal.'"

— *George Mathewson, Senior News Editor, The Observer*
(Sarnia, Ontario)

FIANNA

FIANNA

A story every Canadian school child still learns,
but one conveniently forgotten in America.

Michael Plemmons

First Edition

3A PUBLISHING / CHICAGO

www.3Apublishing.com

For information, please contact 3A Publishing, 744 Cleveland Road, Hinsdale, Illinois,
60521, or ray@mccormackgroup.net.

Printed in the United States of America.
Advanced Review Edition, 2009
First Edition, 2010

ISBN 978-0-9843864-0-6

Library of Congress Control Number: 2010920487

Cover and Book Design by McCormack Group, Inc.
Cover photo courtesy of Vicki Reynolds Mazur.

"The better part of one's life consists of his friendships."
Abraham Lincoln, 1849

This book is for my mother... and for Ray.
Two friends. Two angels.

Contents

Illustrations   *xiii*

Foreword and Acknowledgements   *xxi*

Introduction   *3*

PART ONE: "The greatest army of Irishmen upon which the sun ever shone" — "I suppose I had not seen enough of shot and shell"   *9*

PART TWO: The "curse of Cromwell" and the origin of Atkinson   *27*

PART THREE: "A man who... throws his whole soul into it" — Shouting distance — "Private assurances..." — Sarnia braces for invasion — O'Neill takes command   *43*

PART FOUR: "I gave you five full days" — Shoulder to shoulder — Acquired risk — "Those stormy days" — What "saved Canada for England" — Common cause — "2,000 plump sovereigns"   *75*

PART FIVE: "A big black stallion no one else
could handle"   *109*

PART SIX: The two Irelands: Lunch with
Gladstone and the legacy of Fenianism —
"The Crime of the Century" — Protestants had
a nickname for Home Rule: They called it
Rome Rule — "Untold abominations..." —
"What fools we were"   *119*

ILLUMINATIONS: The Fenian mystique —
A "thousand mile front" — Scapa Flow, 1914:
a measure of Fenian revenge on the Royal Navy —
The Church v. The Fenians — "Not admissible to
the sacraments of the Church" — A page from
Madison's 1812 playbook — The case of
the preoccupied pilot: how to disable a 685-ton
warship blocking your way to Canada   *147*

Bibliography and Further Reading   *171*
Index   *177*

Illustrations

FIRST INSERT

Battle of Ridgeway, 1866 (Library of Congress)
Fenian killed in action, 1870 (Brome County
    Historical Society)
USS Michigan with captured Fenians in tow, 1866
President James Madison (White House Collection)
Secretary of State James Monroe (White House Collection)
General George Meade (Library of Congress)
President Grover Cleveland (Library of Congress)
James Stephens, Irish Republican Brotherhood leader
    (Wikipedia)
William Roberts, Fenian Brotherhood leader
    (Library of Congress)
Allan Pinkerton with Abraham Lincoln, circa 1863
    (Library of Congress)
President Andrew Johnson (Library of Congress)
Secretary of State William Seward (Library of Congress)
John O'Mahony, founder of Fenian Brotherhood
    (Library of Congress)

Captain Raphael Semmes, commander of *CSS Alabama*
    (Getty Images)

General "Fighting Tom" Sweeny (Library of Congress)

Map of Fenian Invasion Plan, 1866 (McCormack/Plemmons)

Map of Fenian Invasion Plan, 1870 (McCormack/Plemmons)

Canadian Cartoon, Jean-Baptiste Côte, 1866
    (Library and Archives Canada)

Second Insert

British Military Officers in Ireland, 1850s (Getty Images)

Oliver Cromwell, 1649 (National Portrait Gallery, London)

Massacre of Drogheda, 1649 (Henry Doyle, 1822-1892)

King Charles I of England, 1649 (Antoon van Dyck, 1599–1641)

Beheading of King Charles I, 1649 (Getty Images)

"Ireland in Chains", period cartoon, 1848 (Wikipedia)

Irish Catholic Peasantry, County Donegal, 1887 (Getty Images)

"Freedom to Ireland", lithograph, 1866 (Currier & Ives)

Forced eviction of Irish tenant-farmer family, 1879 (Wikipedia)

Anti-Irish propaganda cartoon, December, 1867 (Punch Magazine)

Sir Charles Trevelyan, British Asst. Secretary to the Treasury, circa 1848 (Sean Sexton)

Willam Smith O'Brien, Irish nationalist, circa 1848 (Getty Images)

Thomas Francis Meagher, Irish nationalist and commander of the "Fighting 69th" Irish Brigade, circa 1862 (Library of Congress)

National Flag of Ireland (iStockphoto LP)

O'Brien and Meagher under arrest in Dublin, 1848
(Kilmainham Gaol)

"A Terrible Record" (*Weekly Freeman,* July 2, 1881)

Irish Immigrant ships at Quebec's harbor, 1859
(Getty Images)

Memorial to Irish typhus victims at Grosse-Île, Quebec,
1909 (Library and Archives Canada)

Third Insert

Obituary of James J. Atkinson (*Detroit News*, 1940)

O'Brien J. Atkinson, circa 1895 (Port Huron Museum)

Portrait of William Smith O'Brien, circa 1847
(Artist Unknown)

Port Huron, Michigan, by Alfred Ruger, circa 1867
(Library of Congress)

John Atkinson, circa 1867 (The Burton Collection, Detroit
Public Library)

Hazen Pingree, Detroit Mayor and Governor, circa 1896

Company C, 22nd Michigan atop Lookout Mountain, 1863
(Vicki Reynolds Mazur)

Johnny Clem, "Drummer Boy of Chickamauga", circa 1864
(The Pearce Museum at Navarro College)

William F. Atkinson, circa 1900
(*Detroit News*, 1907)

General William Tecumseh Sherman, 1864
(Library of Congress)

Confederate Prison at Danville, 1863
(Library of Congress)

Confederate Units, circa 1863 (Library of Congress)

James J. Atkinson, circa 1938 (The Burton Collection, Detroit
Public Library)

General George Armstrong Custer, circa 1865
    (Library of Congress)
Union forces encamped at Battle of Nashville, 1864
    (Library of Congress)
James Atkinson at high school graduation in Port Huron
    (Port Huron Musuem)
Young Thomas "Al" Edison, Port Huron, circa 1860
    (Library of Congress)
Henry Ford and his prototype automobile, circa 1896
    (© Ford Motor Company)
General Braxton Bragg, CSA, circa 1862 (Library of Congress)
General James Longstreet, CSA, circa 1862
    (Library of Congress)
General George H. Thomas, the "Rock of Chickamauga",
    1863 (Library of Congress)
Officers of the "Fighting 69th" Irish Brigade, 1862
    (Library of Congress)
General James Mulligan, commander of 23rd Illinois Irish
    Brigade, 1862 (Library of Congress)
First Bishop Rev. John McMullen, 1881
    (*The Life and Writings of the Right Reverend John McMullen,
    D. D.* by J. J. McGovern, John Lancaster Spalding)
Detroit, 1870 (Library of Congress)

Fourth Insert

Victoria Rifles on parade, Montreal, 1866
(McCord Museum of Canadian History)

Monument commemorating Battle of Ridgeway, Toronto,
1866 (McCord Museum of Canadian History)

Canadian General Service Medal, Fenian Raid, 1870
(Archives of Ontario Canada)

Thomas D'Arcy McGee, "Father of Confederation", 1867
(McCord Museum of Canadian History)

Funeral of D'Arcy McGee, 1868
(Library and Archives Canada)

Canadian spymaster Gilbert McMicken, circa 1891
(*The Canadian Album: Men of Canada* by W. Cochrane)

Thomas Miller Beach *alias* Henri Le Caron, 1889
(Henri Le Caron Foundation)

Fenian General John O'Neill, 1870 (Historic Omaha)

President Ulysses S. Grant, circa 1870
(Library of Congress)

Colonel John Atkinson on horse, circa 1888 (The Burton
Collection, Detroit Public Library)

Map of Holt County, Nebraska, 1895

Newspaper Ad for Henri Le Caron, M.D., circa 1872
(Henri Le Caron Foundation)

Fenian inventor John P. Holland, 1897 (Wikipedia)

Tombstone of John P. Holland, "Father of the Modern
　　Submarine" (Flickr Commons)

William Gladstone, circa 1890 (Getty Images)

Cartoon by John Porter (*The Weekly Freeman*, 1889)

Colonel John Atkinson, 1893 (The Burton Collection, Detroit
　　Public Library)

Charles Stewart Parnell, Irish statesman, circa 1879
　　(Library of Congress)

Katherine O'Shea, circa 1879
　　(University College Cork, Ireland)

Dr. Patrick Cronin, murdered member of Clan-na-Gael,
　　1889 (Artist Unknown)

Alexander Sullivan of Chicago's Clan-na-Gael, circa 1889
　　(Artist Unknown)

Lord Randolph Churchill, 1893 (Wikipedia)

British Colonial Secretary Winston Churchill, 1900
　　(Library of Congress)

Foreword and Acknowledgements

This book is taken from a much longer work about two extraordinary 19th century immigrant families – the Atkinsons of Michigan and the McMullens of Chicago.

While researching the Atkinsons' involvement with an 1860s-era group known as the Fenians, it became clear this story deserves stand-alone publication.

For most of us who are familiar with the 101 version of American history, this is news. In the politically raucous years immediately following the Civil War, thousands of Union veterans and former Confederate soldiers joined forces to overthrow British rule in Ireland by twice invading British North America: what we call Canada. This incredible episode has been lost in the American consciousness. Today most computer spell-check programs tag the word Fenian as unrecognized. Here and there a few scholars have assayed the subject, but the one book that is still considered the gold standard on Fenianism was published in 1947... as a doctoral thesis.

We hope this narrative will give the Fenians renewed historical life and convey to readers a sense of the astonishment we encountered in research.

This is by no means a comprehensive study of the Fenian movement – our main focus was the Atkinsons and McMullens. But we do include source material which (to the best of our knowledge) is presented for the first time. The undercover Pinkerton investigation of Midwestern Fenian circles has not been detailed elsewhere. We include a rare interview with Fenian commander William Atkinson. Also: a sidebar on the Fenians' long theological battle with the Catholic Church, including a vignette of the Rev. John McMullen and his Fenian friend – the Civil War hero James Mulligan. This, too, is new to Fenian scholarship.

One special note: nothing here is fictionalized or supposed. There are places where a novelist might be tempted to pick up his pen, but we stick to what we can verify – even if it leaves a tantalizing loose thread. Any conjecture is identified as such.

Writing is reading. For a work of this kind, the ratio is one to ten. This writer benefited from indispensible research assistance and – above all – the wisdom and generous support of editor-publisher Ray McCormack. We thank Vicki Reynolds Mazur, a family historian whose dedication over many years has produced a trove of information and insights. And Joe Ann Burgett was a tremendous help sleuthing her way through a mosaic of sources in Detroit and Port Huron.

This is one of many chapters in the kaleidoscopic saga of the Atkinsons and McMullens. It's a project that began two years ago with an inspired remark by Ray McCormack's wife Judy. Within a few months Ray was surprised to find a handful of proud (and probably still frustrated) Fenians in his own family tree.

There might be one or two in yours too.

Michael Plemmons
Cataract, Wisconsin, May 2009

FIANNA

Introduction

On the night of May 21, 1870, a 24-year old former Union army captain and 15 "unwavering" men stepped onto a southbound train in Port Huron, Michigan, and set off to steal Canada. They expected to join 20,000 other "sons of Ireland" in finally realizing the ambition of Jefferson, Madison and Monroe,[1] but their purpose in seizing British North America was altogether different.

The next day in Detroit, William Atkinson's squad was "augmented" by 60 men, barely a full company and far fewer than hoped for. But in Toledo spirits soared as several hundred eager troops clambered aboard the Lake Shore & Michigan Southern train. And then in Cleveland the following day: hundreds more. Many of these men proudly wore their old Union army-issue uniforms, but under those woolen blues they were attired in bright green shirts.

By the time Atkinson's invasion force reached Buffalo two days later, another 500 soldiers were waiting and townspeople

---

1 See page 163: *A page from Madison's 1812 playbook.*

hosted a gala reception. This sizeable regiment now planned to link up with the main body of troops gathering in upstate New York and Vermont.

But four hundred miles away, along the British-Canadian side of the border, professional militia and crack regulars of the Queen's Own – alerted by informers – were already preparing defensive positions. Soon they would learn the precise locations, expected strengths and exact time of invasion. Canadian commanders, who were still smarting from a humiliation four years earlier, would be ready this time.

What follows is a story every Canadian school child still learns, but one that has been largely (perhaps conveniently) forgotten in America.

This is the story of an Irish-American army – at one point 80,000 strong – known as the Fenian Brotherhood. They were the only private military organization ever permitted, actually encouraged, to organize and acquire arms and freely operate within the United States. For a span of five years following the Civil War, the Fenians' support of armed rebellion in Ireland and their outrageous invasions of British North America captivated the nation, enraged the British, panicked Canadians living on the border... and at times forced some artful diplomatic maneuvers to prevent war with England.

For William Atkinson and his brothers, it's a story that ranges from Cromwell's plundering cavalry in the 17th century to an upstart "Irish colony" in 1870s Nebraska. And for William there is a special irony. He may have been the only Fenian to successfully invade Canada – but it was weeks earlier in 1870 and his conquest was a bride named Kate.

As we know, the Fenians did not free Ireland. But arguably they did "liberate" two million mostly-impoverished and mostly-ignored Irish immigrants who were then living in America. And in the process they united – if only for self-defense – a disparate array of British colonies in their first real step toward nationhood.

FIANNA

PART 1

*"The greatest army of Irishmen upon which
the sun ever shone"*

Of the four Atkinson boys Port Huron sent to The War Between The States, William was the last to come home. In 1865 his infantry regiment, the 3rd Michigan, had been transferred to New Orleans and then to Texas[1] as part of occupying Union forces. He finally mustered out in late May, 1866, more than a year after Lee's surrender. On the Fourth of July of that year, a brief notice in the *Port Huron Press* announced the return of a favorite son.

"Wm. Atkinson has seen considerable service and endured much of the hardships of war," the newspaper said. "He has hosts of friends here who warmly welcome his return."

Four years earlier the 16-year old William – lean and scrappy with a dry sense of humor – had enlisted in the 22nd Michigan as an infantry private. He came back wearing captain's bars: a former signal officer on Sherman's staff, a

---

1 Texas formally rejoined the Union in March 1870. Georgia was the last state to be readmitted, in July of that year.

local legend for his escape from a Confederate prison and 300-mile odyssey through the West Virginia wilderness back to Union lines.

William made his reputation in a single afternoon at Chickamauga in 1863. As a sergeant he retrieved the fallen regimental flag at Horseshoe Ridge (shot out from under two color bearers only seconds earlier) while wrapping his own leg wound and rallying Company C for another charge by Longstreet's corps.[1] Chickamauga was tactically a Union defeat, but battlefield historians agree that by holding the battered right flank for three hours the 22nd Michigan and two Ohio units saved a confused Rosecrans and the main body of his retreating army from a rout – perhaps a collapse of the western offensive.[2]

An older brother, Patrick Atkinson, was captured with William at Chickamauga. Patrick remains in the former Confederacy under a plain marker at Andersonville, Georgia,

---

1   This summary is from a detailed regimental history.

2   Union forces regrouped near Chattanooga and eventually secured that vital transportation hub. The cost was high. Of more than 16,000 Union casualties, virtually all the 22nd Michigan was captured or killed alongside that now-famous creek. The stand of the 22nd is well known to Civil War scholars but not the general public, and it is controversial. Some veterans never forgave Rosecrans for "leaving us on the field."

one of 12,913 Union prisoners who died there.

Another older brother, John, 25, entered service as a captain in 1861. He mustered out as a Lieutenant Colonel early in 1866 and brought home to Port Huron a wife he'd met while stationed in San Antonio – Lida Lyons, the daughter of a Confederate surgeon and mayor of the city. Like many men who achieved field-grade rank during the war, "Colonel" became an honorific for the rest of John's life.[3]

John in fact had commanded Company C through several minor engagements in the year leading up to Chickamauga. And there is no doubt, given his reckless passion for confrontation, the only reason he survived the battle was he'd been summoned to division headquarters just prior to Bragg's surprise advance. So decimated was the 22nd that then-Captain John Atkinson was ordered back to Michigan to recruit a new regiment (even as the family mourned Patrick and William, their fates unknown at the time.)

Younger brother James (a boyhood pal of "Al" Edison in the waterfront Ward One neighborhood of Port Huron) had joined the 3rd Michigan when he came of age in 1865. He too

---

3 Colonel John wasted no time capitalizing on his new status. He was appointed the Customs Inspector for Port Huron and already was active in local politics by the time William returned from the war.

was safely home.

A fifth brother, O'Brien, enlisted in the 2nd Michigan cavalry but his regiment never mustered in. Michigan by then had met all its quotas, totaling some 91,000 soldiers (14,000 were killed or died of disease). During the war O'Brien was twice elected prosecutor for St. Clair County, including Port Huron, in 1862 and again in 1864, and quickly became one of the area's influential figures.

All four surviving Atkinson brothers – O'Brien, John, William and James – became celebrated lawyers, judges, politicians. Streets and schools and parks would be named for Atkinsons. Fifty years later they would be referred to by a *Detroit News* writer as "that gallant quartet" who shaped Michigan politics and national history in the second half of 19th century, not to mention filling untold columns of newsprint with scandal. They were, as reporters like to say, good copy. And for a town the size of Port Huron in the late 1860s, population roughly 5,500, they had already established a powerful brand.

But there is a much larger context here. By 1865 the Atkinsons were only four among more than 150,000 well-trained Catholic Irish soldiers in the various Union armies – by far the largest (white) minority group in uniform. Three-quarters of these men were Irish-born and had immigrated less than a generation earlier. Some were still learning English as a second language (and more comfortable speaking Gaelic).

These Catholic Irish veterans shared a new sense of confidence and belonging in their adopted homeland (albeit a homeland that had not entirely adopted *them*).

They also shared a blood grievance far transcending this American conflict.

Three years before the war, on St. Patrick's Day in 1858, an organization know as the Fenian Brotherhood was formed in New York City. Its sole purpose was the military overthrow of British rule on that "imprisoned island" known as Ireland. The Fenians dreamed of fielding a massive army of Celtic warriors (hence the name, taken from the "Fianna" of Irish mythology) to turn back the clock on Cromwell and vanquish the "Saxon vampire."

This dream-army was to be raised on Irish soil and fight under the banner of the Irish Republican Brotherhood. The Fenians' role in America was to send material support and funding – what leaders called the "sinews of war" – and perhaps volunteer brigades.

Initially, support was slow. Most immigrant Catholic Irish, concentrated in the slums of large cities such as Boston, New York and Chicago, were far more concerned with economic survival in a new nation where "No Irish Need Apply" was a familiar storefront sign. Irish liberation was a misty ideal, an old cudgel, a reminder of the defeated conditions they'd escaped. Catholic immigrants had seen countless futile risings, always easily crushed and punctuated with the usual round of hangings or "transportations" – most recently in the pitiable Young Ireland revolt in 1848, shattered in less than a day.

But then the Civil War broke out. Young Irish men in northern cities enlisted en masse. One: for the income. Two: for an unparalleled chance to elevate their status and prove their patriotism.

So-called Irish Brigades, often named for national heroes such as Robert Emmet or Daniel O'Connell, demonstrated a near-perverse indifference to casualties. The famous "Fighting 69th" of New York City, led by Irish nationalist Thomas Meagher, sustained horrific losses at Fredericksburg and Antietam, yet never had a shortage of new recruits.[1] (The 69th is said to have been given its nickname by an awestruck Robert E. Lee.)

Another renowned unit was the 23rd Illinois Irish Brigade, organized and commanded by Colonel James Mulligan of

---

1 Casualty rates up to 25% were common in major Civil War engagements, but at Antietam the Fighting 69th lost more than 60% of its regimental strength attacking the entrenched Confederate center. At Fredericksburg, another Union rout, Irish Brigade losses were far higher: the 69th was reduced from 1,600 to 256. Irish nationalist leaders had hoped America's civil war would instruct and harden Irish-American soldiers for the coming crusade against England – but it turned out Union commanders were the ones most in need of instruction.

Chicago. He would have figured large in Fenian leadership after the war – had he survived. We mention him here because Mulligan was the boyhood friend of future Archbishop John McMullen and it was McMullen, ironically a sworn enemy of Fenianism, who gave the eulogy when Mulligan was killed in 1864 (more about this later.)[2]

IN MANY WAYS, the Civil War empowered the Irish in America as no other social or economic event could. That is to say, the Catholic Irish. In Ireland they had once been forbidden to own personal weapons or even a horse of military quality, forced to worship in small churches made of wood (for convenient burning by Protestant authorities in case of a rising), forbidden to own lands or vote or marry a Protestant. But in America between 1861 and 1865 Catholic immigrants shook off many of the old stereotypes that had confined their ambitions. The war transformed their prospects.

By 1865 the British authorities in Ireland were closing in

---

2   One generation later, the daughter of McMullen's brother James would marry a son of the Fenian William Atkinson, linking these two illustrious families.

on the IRB[1], but for Fenian leaders in America the situation couldn't have seemed more promising: membership soared; donations poured in. Against all odds, a great Catholic Irish army had been summoned into existence (although technically it was under a different command structure.) The Union cause had built the Fenians' army for them.[2]

Rather than having to dodge between safe houses, Fenian leaders were treated like celebrities. President John O'Mahony held grandiose press conferences at Moffat Mansion in New York City. Newspapers in Boston, Chicago and Philadelphia, with their thousands of Irish readers, competed for exclusives. Against a background of intense anti-British feeling after the Civil War, a kind of populist Fenian chic developed.

At an ecstatic rally in Buffalo, New York, Fenian leader William Roberts vowed to send into the field "the greatest Army of Irishmen upon which the sun ever shone." And soon.

---

1   In the fall of 1865 – like clockwork – the IRB was smashed in a series of raids by special units of British police (who by now were experts in planting spies and subverting insurrections). The police rounded up more than 150 leaders, including several Irish Catholic Americans, and intercepted a Fenian-chartered vessel – *Erin's Hope* – loaded with arms, men and ammunition. It was shades of 1848. Everything now depended on the American Fenians.

2   As Union veterans mustered out, they were allowed to purchase their military-issue rifles or muskets for as little as $6. Many did so.

"I suppose I had not seen enough of shot and shell."

Port Huron after the Civil War was known for a signature sound that could be heard miles upriver... and across the way in Canada. Edison remembered it from his boyhood as an incessant gnawing "hum" of enormous circular and vertical blades. More than a dozen screaming saw mills – many powered by new steam-driven machines – operated from first light to last along the busy Black and St. Clair riverfronts.

The city was in the midst of a timber boom as Michigan in the late 1860s became the nation's primary source for construction-grade lumber.[3] Some of the dirt streets were not

---

3   The once-abundant forests of Maine and upstate New York were by this time nearly exhausted but Michigan, the next state west in the northern "pine belt," was still rich in oak and white pine, the two most economical and in-demand woods for 19th century home builders.

yet named, nor were all the houses numbered, but what once had been little more than a trading post now boasted a couple of small shipyards, two feisty newspapers, a large bank, a rail line, even a high school.

Lumber-cutting wasn't the only noisy enterprise in Port Huron.

The first reported local Fenian meeting was February 19, 1866. A brief item in the *Port Huron Press* said the assembly, at Stewart's Hall, was loud and crowded. And when "a Mr. Verdon of Detroit" took the podium for a two-hour lecture on the history of Irish oppression by the British, the uninterested *Press* reporter quickly ducked out – claiming "other duties called us away."[1]

Fenians could be pedantic. But seldom were they boring. Only a few weeks later the same newspaper was devoting lengthy accounts to a "Fenian Scare" back East... a run-up to the first invasion of Canada.

That initial gathering was organized and "chaired" by O'Brien Atkinson, one of 11 children and the precocious middle son of James and Elizabeth, who'd emigrated from

---

1 Lawrence Verdon was "foreign secretary" of the Fenian "government-in-exile." He'd come to Port Huron on a recruiting mission.

Canada to Port Huron in 1854[2] – by paying a few pennies and taking a ferry across the St. Clair River. Six years later O'Brien became the first graduate of the new University of Michigan Law School. He had recently been elected prosecutor for St. Clair County.

Eventually the Atkinson-Port Huron "circle" grew to roughly four hundred men, almost all of them immigrants of Irish Catholic descent.[3] Membership required a Fenian sponsor and seconding nomination. Members swore an elaborate oath of "obedience to orders from superior officers." In essence, each Fenian was a "soldier" and was assigned a military rank

---

2   For almost 10 years after the Civil War only New York City surpassed Port Huron as the gateway to America. More than 300,000 immigrants passed through the city from Ontario. The chief reason for this phenomenon: ocean passage to Canada was far less expensive.

To encourage settlement of the North American provinces, the British Passenger Acts reduced fares to Canada to only 15 shillings, compared to a 4- or 5-pound ticket to New York. Protestant Irish landlords, to "clear" their lands of unwanted renters, often subsidized fares or paid for them outright. Thousands of Catholic Irish immigrants disembarked at Halifax, as James and Elizabeth Atkinson did in 1832, and migrated slowly across the Ontario "frontier" for greater opportunities in America.

3   Membership rolls for the Port Huron circle have been lost; this number is conservatively estimated from contemporary accounts of attendance at meetings.

(most were Civil War veterans). Initiation fee was one dollar. Weekly dues were a dime. Not cheap, but in reach for most Irish laborers in Port Huron's saw mills.[1]

There were nine Fenian circles in Michigan, including Detroit and Bay City. By comparison, Massachusetts had 65 (concentrated in the Boston area). Illinois had 26 (mostly in Chicago). There were Fenian circles in Tennessee (4), in Ohio (22) and faraway California (13). Even the recently-admitted state of Nevada had three groups.

With their headquarters in New York City, the Fenians claimed 600 circles around the country. Actual dues-paying membership was always a question. For public relations

---

1   Lumbering was (and still is) lethal work, but it paid well. Young single men spent entire winters in the timberlands: cutting, hauling and piling logs. Typical pay was $25 per month with room and board provided. (River drivers generally earned more, so often were they injured or killed.) Saw mill workers in Port Huron – many of them specialists – commanded wages up to $50 per month, but no room and board. Nor, of course, health benefits. Local newspapers routinely reported severed hands and arms.

By the turn of the 20th century, much of the Midwest had been built from Michigan oak and white pine. Production peaked in 1889 at 5.5 billion board-feet – enough to build half a million homes. Forest fires in 1871 (the same year as the Great Chicago Fire) almost annihilated the lumber industry for cities such as Port Huron, Muskegon and Bay City, but production steadily increased elsewhere in the state.

purposes, figures such as 200,000 were given to reporters. Experts believe 80,000 is a more realistic number.

But in the late 1860s it was the rambunctious Port Huron circle that generated out-size anxiety for officials in Washington, London and Ottawa[2]. What worried them was 1) the city's easy proximity to Sarnia and western Ontario and 2) the Atkinson brothers: O'Brien, John and William.

And what on earth did Canada have to do with Irish oppression? Only that it was British and within striking distance. (We'll explain in a moment.)

In the summer of 1866 a regiment of 2,000 Fenians under Colonel John O'Neill had crossed into Canada from Buffalo. They skirmished with a brigade of stunned militia and then British regulars at Ridgeway and Fort Erie, routing the Canadians twice – then spent more than a full day meandering around the Niagara Peninsula, short of ammunition and supplies, waiting for reinforcements that never came. A trans-Atlantic crisis ensued. Ministers in Ottawa fired off furious cables to Washington where the Johnson administration seemed peculiarly uninterested. Only the Fenians' poor

---

2   In succeeding chapters we'll explain the U. S. government's "double game" with regard to the Fenians – on one hand selling to them large inventories of surplus arms and munitions from federal arsenals, but on the other using spies to stay abreast of their "secret" plans.

logistics and the belated intervention of federal troops under George Meade, of Gettysburg fame, averted possible war with England.

The Atkinson brothers arrived at Fenianism too late for Ridgeway. But rumors and recent events were pointing toward another bolder attempt.

John and William were war heroes "popular among all classes of the community" in Port Huron. O'Brien was re-elected county prosecutor in 1868. Ahead of them lay extraordinary political and legal careers. But it could be said the Atkinsons – more than most Irish immigrants – felt they had unfinished business with England.

Their grandmother Lucy O'Brien (Elizabeth's mother) was a cousin of the 1848 revolutionist William Smith O'Brien – for whom O'Brien was named. And their father had taken part in the doomed Mackenzie's Rebellion in Canada in 1837.[1] Details are scarce, but James's role probably explains

---

1 Also known as the Patriot War, the origins of Mackenzie's Rebellion are complex. It was in essence a short-lived movement for the "independence" of Ontario, a kind of peasant revolt that evolved into an armed "march" on Toronto, quickly and brutally put down by British regulars. As in Ireland, severe economic discrimination in Canada was a matter of law. After the War of 1812, a system of "Crown reserves" restricted ownership of the desirable lands to a wealthy "loyalist" elite. Mackenzie escaped and, after years of exile in the sympathetic United States, eventually was pardoned.

why the family relocated from Toronto (where O'Brien was born) to Lambton County, Ontario. James and Elizabeth were unusually well-educated for the time – James attended college in Limerick, where they'd met. The politics of Irish liberation was standard kitchen-table talk for the Atkinsons.

All three brothers were still in their 20s. And all three naturally expected to play leading roles in the next great conflict – against Britain.[2]

Years later William would tell a Detroit newspaper reporter, "I was young... and I suppose I had not seen enough of shot and shell."

---

2   James, the youngest of the "quartet," returned to school after the war and did not play a prominent role with the Fenians. In 1869 he was among the first graduating class (a class of four) of Port Huron High School. He would go on to study abroad and become the legal scholar of the family.

BATTLE OF RIDGEWAY, C.W.

(Above) Sometimes called "the battle that made Canada," defeat at Ridgeway was a shock for provincial Canadian leaders. It proved not only the folly of relying on scattered and under-strength British garrisons for self-defense, but the incompetence of poorly-trained local Canadian militias. At the time, no more than 8,000 British regulars were stationed in the whole of Canada. Ridgeway provided the political impetus for Canadian Confederation in 1868, and the development of a full-time, professional militia.

When the Fenians attempted another invasion in 1870, Canadians were waiting and ready.

This rendering is a fanciful version of actual proceedings at Ridgeway. A company of Queen's Own Rifles and several terrified Canadian militia units marched south from Toronto to engage a formation of perhaps 1,000 Fenians just west of Fort Erie. What turned the battle was when a Canadian officer saw several Fenians on horseback and assumed a cavalry charge was imminent. He ordered his troops into a tight square – the standard 19th century defense against cavalry – but succeeded only in making them easier targets for Fenian ex-Civil War infantry. In a hail of fire, Canadian units broke and ran.

The Fenians had no cavalry at Ridgeway. Those few horses were "borrowed" from nearby farms.

Plate 1

(*Above*) Fenian killed in action on a roadway near Eccles Hill, Quebec, during 1870 invasion of Canada. (*Below*) Artist sketch of captured Fenians being towed aboard a barge after they were intercepted by the three-masted, iron-hulled frigate *USS Michigan*, 1866.

Plate 2

The idea of seizing Canadian territory as a "bargaining chip" against the British did not originate with the Fenians – this was President James Madison's strategy more than 50 years earlier in the War of 1812. Lacking a serious American navy, Madison *(left)* and his Secretary of State James Monroe *(right)* staked everything on a ground conquest of lightly-defended Ontario. Like the Fenians in 1866, America confidently declared war on Britain – and promptly bungled it. (See the 1866 invasion map on the following pages and "A page from Madison's playbook," page 163.)

(Left) General George Meade (the hero of Gettysburg) led a belated intervention against the Fenians in 1866. By the time he arrived with a small contingent, the invasion of Canada had already self-destructed. *(Right)* Future president Grover Cleveland, then a Buffalo attorney, seized on the chance to make national headlines by representing – pro bono – O'Neill and other Fenian officers who were held for trial. In a deal with the British, charges were later dismissed.

Plate 3

James Stephens *(above left)* and John O'Mahony were among a handful of leaders who escaped the British dragnet after Ireland's disastrous 1848 rising. While in exile in Paris they began to focus on America, with its millions of embittered immigrant Irish, as the great arsenal of money, materiel and manpower for future rebellion.

In the late 1850s, Stephens slipped back into Ireland while O'Mahony arrived in New York. In 1859, they formed a trans-Atlantic partnership: the Irish Republican Brotherhood in Dublin and the Fenian Brotherhood based in New York. The Fenians were able to raise "invasion funds," organize and acquire arms far from the constant glare of landlords, British police and spies. Meanwhile in Ireland the IRB secretly recruited manpower. Ultimately the IRB and Fenians planned to join forces in a "final call" on Irish soil.

When the Civil War broke out, Irish leaders recognized it as a priceless opportunity to organize and train (at government expense) Irish-American soldiers for the crusade to come. A number of large Fenian "circles" enlisted en masse and "Irish brigades" were mustered on both sides of the conflict. By war's end, Fenian leaders believed their time was at hand. But in fall of 1865, once again, British police struck preemptively – arresting Stephens and decimating the IRB in Ireland.

At this point, Fenian leadership in America fractured. O'Mahony wanted time to rebuild. But others, such as William Roberts *(above right)* favored immediate action against the nearest British target: Canada. The Roberts "wing" prevailed.

Plate 4

Allan Pinkerton *(above left)* provided security for Abraham Lincoln at his first inauguration, later became the first chief of Union military intelligence (with mixed results), and operated the world's first private detective and security-service agency in New York City. His agency would later become famous for pursuing Butch Cassidy and the Sundance Kid, and infamous for breaking labor strikes, but in the late 1860s – with the U. S. government as his top client – Pinkerton's primary focus was the Fenian Brotherhood.

Pinkerton recruited a cadre of highly motivated Protestant Irish spies to track the plans and movements of Catholic Irish Fenian leaders in Chicago, Detroit and Port Huron. In his 1868 report, Pinkerton anticipated an invasion of Ontario – led by the Atkinsons – via Port Huron.

Plate 5

President Andrew Johnson *(above left)* and Secretary of State William
Seward *(above right)* tacitly encouraged the Fenians' public threats to invade
British North America – not so much in sympathy for the Irish cause, but
as political leverage against Britain in settling war claims.

(Right)
John O'Mahony, founder
of the Fenian Brotherhood,
was a scholar of linguistics
and veteran of the failed
1848 rising in Ireland.
O'Mahony was unable to
manage the volatile tempers
and schisms within his new
Irish American organization.
He never really believed in
the "Canada scheme" and
died virtually penniless
and forgotten in a New
York boarding house.

Plate 6

(Above) Captain Raphael Semmes (foreground), commander of the *CSS Alabama.* Built in a British shipyard for the Confederacy during the Civil War, the raider sank or captured nearly 70 Union or Union-chartered vessels. After victory in 1865, an incensed United States Congress and the Johnson administration demanded reparations from England – Senator Charles Sumner insisted the British either pay $2 billion or cede all of Canada. Two years after the last Fenian raid on Canada, the British finally settled war claims for U.S. $15.5 million.

(Left)
General "Fighting Tom" Sweeny, decorated veteran of Shiloh, was the Fenian Secretary of War and architect of the 1866 Fenian invasion. Sweeny's plan (see map on following page) called for as many as 50,000 battle-hardened Irish-American soldiers to overwhelm a British-Canadian force of amateur militia and 8,000 regulars dispersed across the provinces.

Plate 7

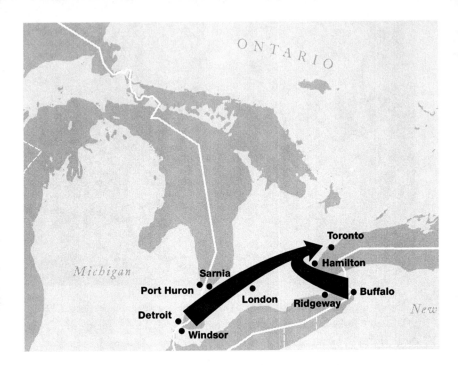

A "thousand mile front": the 1866 Invasion Plan:

Early in 1866, at the Fenian convention in Pittsburgh, "Secretary of War" General Thomas Sweeny presented this basic outline for the conquest of Ontario and seizure of the St Lawrence Seaway. The plan called for three simultaneous crossings in force: 1) from Detroit to Windsor, then east-northeast to London and Toronto, 2) from Buffalo to the Niagara peninsula, then north to Hamilton and Toronto, and 3) from Vermont into Quebec province, then west to Ottawa.

The western and central Fenian armies would converge near Toronto, then drive northeast to meet their comrades at Ottawa. In a matter of days, Great Britain (and the world) would be confronted with the "accomplished facts."

Except for the Vermont aspect, Sweeny's concept was virtually identical to invasion plans of President James Madison when the United States declared war on Britain in 1812 – rapid pincer movements leading to the collapse of outnumbered British North American forces.

Madison's invasion by poorly-led militia was a disaster, as the Fenians well knew. But unlike 1812, in 1866 the Fenians could muster thousands of ex-Union infantry and officers – straight from the battlefields of the Civil

Plate 8

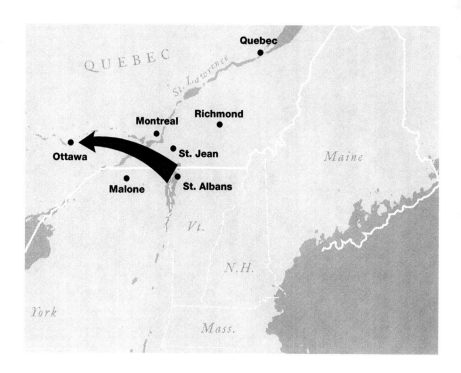

War. Sweeny justifiably believed his triple-wing offensive would overwhelm the limited resources of untested Canadian militia and small garrisons of British regulars. What's more, Fenian leaders had been led to believe they would have a free hand – the U. S. government would not interfere.

But delays revealed the fatal flaw: logistics.

The original concept presumed a winter campaign, when rivers were frozen and passable. But as arguments within Fenian leadership dragged into the spring of 1866 – as the winter ice thawed – Sweeny's 10,000-man plan grew increasingly complex. Another crossing, by ferry from Cleveland, was added. Then a fifth assault point along the Quebec border.

Eventually, planners expected as many as 50,000 troops to converge (clandestinely) from 22 states at a dozen start points – all this via a dubious transportation system of steam engine and coach, with coordination by telegraph and courier. Only 5,000 to 7,000 Fenians ever reached their designated start points, most of them long after O'Neill had crossed at Buffalo on June 1, 1866. This doomed any chance of O'Neill following up his victory at Ridgeway.

Plate 9

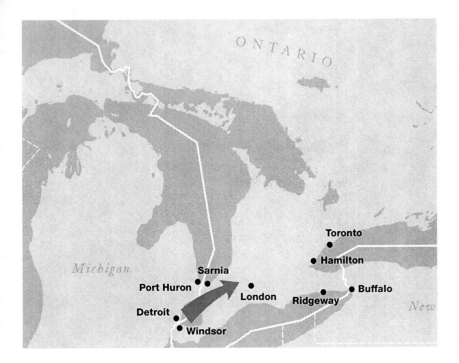

Round Two: the 1870 plan:

Four years after his first excursion on Canadian soil, O'Neill was calling all the shots in 1870. He stripped the Fenian invasion plan down to its one essential element: seizure of the St. Lawrence. Conquest and occupation of Ontario (the goal in 1866) would be irrelevant once Fenians controlled the commercial lifeline between Canada and Britain. Equally important, fortified Fenian artillery positions on the southern banks of the St. Lawrence would be near-impregnable against any Canadian or British counterattacks.

With an expected 20,000 troops, O'Neill planned a two-pronged crossing from far northeastern New York State (near Malone) and St. Albans, Vermont. He would capture the towns of St. Jean, just south of Montreal, and Richmond, nestled against the Green Mountains, then occupy the sparsely-populated but vital region between the St. Lawrence and the American border (shaded area) – again, presuming official indifference from the U. S. government.

Plate 10

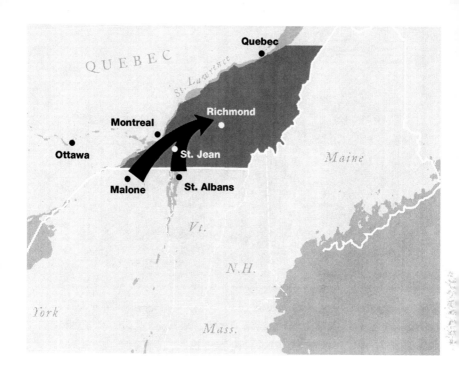

O'Neill still needed a western flank in 1870, but this time as a diversion. He reasoned that Canadian leaders, with their bitter memories of 1866, would instantly dispatch reinforcements to any reported crossing from Detroit (a Port Huron-to-Sarnia crossing was ruled out). Accordingly, the Fenians' "Michigan Division" would invade Windsor, commandeer rail transport and fight its way eastward to join O'Neill's army in lower Quebec.

Sources are not clear on exactly how the Michigan Division would accomplish this 900-kilometer feat… with London, Toronto and Ottawa in the way. And it seems that large numbers of Fenian rank and file were not clear on this point either. Hundreds of expected troops failed to report and the diversionary attack never materialized.

Command passed to William F. Atkinson, who was left to scramble eastward by rail, collecting stranded Fenian units along the way, to join O'Neill in New York – too late.

Plate 11

This astute 1866 Canadian cartoon by Jean-Baptiste Côte' depicts Uncle Sam threatening to unleash his attack dog (the Fenians) on innocent Canada if John Bull (Britain) fails to pay war reparations demanded by the United States.

Throughout the first half of the 19th century, Americans imbued with "Manifest Destiny" coveted large regions of British-Canadian territory. In 1844-46, the two nations almost went to war again (for what would have been the third time in 70 years) over the disputed Oregon territory until a compromise set the 49th parallel as the border, ceding Washington and Oregon to America. During the Civil War, rebel incursions from across the Canadian border further strained relations.

Considering attitudes and events of the preceding few decades, the Fenians had reason to believe the American government would support (or at least sanction) their plans.

At the time of the first Fenian invasion in 1866, British North America was a loose collection of sibling provinces (just as our American colonies had been in 1776). Confederation of the provinces under British rule had been discussed but was politically stalled – that is, until O'Neill's unmolested crossing demonstrated just how easily the whole of Canada might be conquered if not for America's lack of coordinated interest.

Within two years, Ontario, Quebec and other eastern provinces – with Britain's urging and approval – voted to Confederate in a self-governing Home Rule model. Britain retained sovereignty in diplomatic and defense matters. (Ironically, this was identical to the Home Rule model Gladstone wanted to give Ireland decades later).

Plate 12

PART 2

The "curse of Cromwell" and the origin of Atkinson

The reader will recall our mentioning a bored Port Huron newspaperman who fled a Fenian assembly when the speaker launched into a two-hour discourse on Irish history. We should not repeat that mistake.

But neither shall we need two hours.

To really understand the defining imprint of this "blood grievance" the Atkinsons and all Irish Catholics felt in the 19th century, a brief survey is worthwhile. Most writers on Fenianism trace its origin to a failed Irish revolt in 1848 (since Fenian founder John O'Mahony was one of the leaders). But this is like dating the American civil rights struggle to Martin Luther King – leaving the matter of slavery to presumed foreknowledge.

In fact, Irish slavery is a significant but little-known part of this story.

But first, we have a mystery to consider.

Atkinson is not a typically Irish Catholic name. Genealogists say this surname originated in northern England and Scotland about the time of the Norman conquests in the 11th century. Atkinson is more commonly rendered as Acheson in Scotland. A glance through British history – British, not Irish – reveals many notable Atkinsons. The only venue in Irish history where one discovers Atkinsons is Ulster. Atkinsons were among the wealthy and politically-connected "planters" who took vast land holdings confiscated from Catholic clans after the Elizabethan conquest, around 1600.

Virtually all of these Atkinsons were Protestant. So how is it we find a bootstrapping immigrant family of Catholic Atkinsons in Port Huron, Michigan, in the 1860s?

Clues are few. A brief line in the *Cyclopedia of Michigan* (published in 1900) said: "The family are (sic) supposed to be of English origin and were intensely Protestant during the time of Oliver Cromwell, but soon became and still are Roman Catholic… and enthusiastic (Irish) nationalists." No attribution. Nothing further.

Somewhere an Atkinson went native – converted from either the Anglican or Presbyterian faith to Catholicism. Today we would think of this as perhaps a convenience for marriage. But in the immediate post-Cromwell era this was a decision that ensured excoriating civil punishments and absolute social opprobrium. It was tantamount to treason.

Under a set of Penal Laws known as The Growth of Popery Act (designed to kill growth, not promote it), any Protestant who converted to Catholicism instantly forfeited all lands and legal rights. The act specifies that such an individual could "remain in prison at the monarch's pleasure" and "no injury – however atrocious – could have any action brought against it or any reparation for such."

There was no percentage in converting to Catholicism. Political, social and economic tides were all running the other way. Even many prominent Irish Catholics were adopting a Protestant nameplate (to save what lands were left to them).

What woman or what passion led one of his forebears to this extraordinary act of faith (or love), we can only speculate. What we do know is this: James Atkinson was born in 1800, in County Mayo, a Catholic. He met Elizabeth Shinners, also a Catholic, while attending college in Limerick. And in 1832 they departed Ireland for the promise of a better life in Canada.

Although in Ireland he was a civil engineer and surveyor, James encountered much the same anti-Catholic discrimination in the New World. For years in eastern Ontario he could find only pick-and-shovel work. Family biographers say at one point he was earning a nickel an hour clearing land for development by wealthy Protestant settlers.[1]

As children came, the Atkinsons moved steadily west

---

1   It's easy to understand why, in later years, the Atkinson boys were obsessed with acquiring and "churning" real estate, from Port Huron to Detroit, Mackinac to Bois Blanc... even Nebraska. (Port Huron newspapers in the 1860s and '70s are dotted with frequent Atkinson real estate transactions.)

across Ontario, eventually settling near Sarnia where James secured work surveying. O'Brien, a middle son, had been born in Toronto. William, six years his junior, was born in Warwick. Verifiable reminiscences from this period are hard to come by. John was said to remember attending church services in his bare feet. Another family story tells of mother Elizabeth carrying one of the younger children to school through a blizzard... on her back.[1]

Meanwhile, across the St. Clair River in America, Port Huron was enjoying explosive prosperity from the timber trade and shipbuilding. In 1854, three years before Port Huron was incorporated, the Atkinsons boarded a ferry at Sarnia and took up residence near the waterfront (also home to the family of Samuel Edison, just arrived from Ohio).

Later accounts say James was beginning to have "substantial" success in the lumber business when he died in 1856. Elizabeth survived him by three decades – long enough to witness not only the Civil War but the astonishing self-made success of her sons.

---

1   As famously noted by Tolstoy and instinctively understood by all, every family has its creation myth. For later generations, unverifiable facts are less important than a shared belief in their meaning.

CONSIDERING ALL OF THIS, let's take a look now – through Fenian eyes – at the English Civil Wars of the 17th century.

In 1649, only a few months after the English parliament deposed and beheaded Charles I, a mercenary expedition under Cromwell crossed the Irish Sea to settle accounts. They "re-conquered" and over the next 10 years systematically emasculated Ireland. Almost all Catholic-owned lands were seized and awarded to Protestant Scottish and English investors. Priests were executed, churches burned, practice of the faith banned – all in reprisal for the Irish confederation's disastrous royalist alliance.

The campaign was a savage, once-and-for-all proposition. Villages and towns that resisted were singled out for near extermination. In the fortified port cities, such as Drogheda and Wexford, where well-armed Catholic garrisons held out for weeks, capitulation was met with indiscriminate slaughter and looting. Between 1651 and 1660 an estimated 130,000 Catholic Irish – many of them children – were auctioned into slavery in the English settlements of America and the West Indies.[2]

---

2   Many readers will be shocked by this information. The story of Catholic Irish slavery in the 17th century has long since been eclipsed by the African holocaust. But the records are clear. At least 100,000 Catholic children age 10 to 14 were sold as slaves (sometimes identified as indentured servants) and shipped to British colonies in Virginia, New England and the West Indies during the 1650s.

Massacres and mass dispossession were not new in Ireland. But the 12th century Normans had never really controlled the countryside. Eventually they were smitten with and assimilated into the culture. Even after the Elizabethan conquests, and creation of a hated plantation system, much of Ireland was still nominally owned and governed by native Gaelic-speaking Catholics.

This time was different. Cromwell's victory was comprehensive. And he brooked no accommodations with the old Catholic clan leaders. Confiscation of lands was codified in an Act of Settlement, followed by Penal Laws outlining new death-penalty offenses and forbidding Catholics ever to vote or hold public office.

Virtually overnight Ireland was transformed – for native Catholics – into an apartheid state. Before Cromwell, Catholics still owned 60% of all property in Ireland. Less than a century later: only 5%. In what today would be condemned as ethnic cleansing, thousands of farmers were deported to the ruined soils of Connaught Province, and their rich lands in eastern Ireland occupied by Protestant settlers and former soldiers.

Ten years later, Cromwell was dead (probably from malaria contracted during his Irish campaign) and The Protectorate too. Restoration of the English crown brought a measure of tolerance. Irish Catholics were allowed to worship publicly again. Hundreds of surviving priests returned from exile.

But any hopes that Catholic-owned lands might also be restored were soon quashed. Considering the fate of his father, Charles II was not of a mind to confront the newly-installed Protestant gentry of Ireland and their investors in Britain.

What was done was done.

A Penal Law sampler

In what became known as the Ascendancy, the next generation of Protestant landowners in Ireland solidified their grip on power with a new set of Penal Laws in 1695 – confirming and extending Cromwell's original prohibitions. Among the many provisions:

Catholics and dissenters banned from serving in the Irish Parliament (rescinded in 1829).

Intermarriage with Protestants forbidden (repealed in 1778).

Inheritance of Catholic-owned land (generally tracts of fewer than 15 acres) must be subdivided equally between all an owner's sons (ensuring that successive generations would own increasingly less land). The notable exception was if the eldest son converted to Anglicism – at which point he became the sole owner.

Priests required to register with local magistrates. When allowed, new Catholic churches to be built only from wood – not stone – and away from main roads.

Catholics forbidden to own firearms (rescinded in 1793), nor a horse valued at more than 5 pounds.

HISTORIANS DEBATE WHETHER the Penal Laws were intended to crush "popery" by coercing conversion or simply enforce political control. Does it matter? Most of the old Catholic aristocracy had long since faced facts and converted to state-sponsored Anglicism. A handful of politically-connected Catholics such as the Earl of Antrim did manage to retain ancestral lands. But the overwhelming majority of Catholics – the tenant farmers, laborers, shopkeepers and professionals (of what emerged as a new middle class) – never gave up the faith.

Catholic political leaders often complained, however, that the faith gave up on *them*. In a twist that would have pleased Henry VIII, the Vatican consistently "recognized" Anglican supremacy in order to be allowed to retain its priests and churches in Ireland. And as we will see, outside of individual renegade priests, the Church avoided any involvement in independence movements it felt were futile and threatened the status quo. Such was the moral vise of English occupation.

As their natural rights evaporated and landlords "screwed up" (Swift's words) the rents, Catholics turned to secret societies and insurgencies. Authorities retaliated with forced evictions of any and all suspect families. The first of countless post-Cromwell famines, in 1651, was largely self-engineered by landlords – backed by British bayonets – destroying crops and livestock of tenant farmers. Which in turn beget more murder and arson.[1]

Thus the cycle began.

Some writers have compared the Irish experience under English domination to that of the American colonies. It's a tempting analogy. But we must remember that our colonies were thousands of miles distant from a "mother country," and they enjoyed substantial economic and governmental freedoms. Ireland was a militarily-conquered nation whose

---

1 It's important to remember the American Fenians were not saboteurs or Molly Maguire-style assassins. Not for them were hit and run tactics. These were military men, a unique product of the Civil War. They thought in terms of large troop deployments, maneuver and decisive engagement. Honor on the battlefield and chivalry mattered.

In reports after the battle of Ridgeway in 1866, in which nine young Canadian militiamen were killed and a like number of Fenians died, even defeated Canadian officers said the Fenian invaders behaved "with courtesy" while on Canadian soil: no looting, no harassment of locals. One of the more bizarre sidelights of Ridgeway was an official Fenian Proclamation handed out to alarmed Canadian civilians:

"To the People of British North America, we come among you as the foes of British rule in Ireland. We have taken up the sword to strike down the oppressors' rod, to deliver Ireland from the tyrant, the despoiler, the robber. We have no issue with the people of these Provinces and wish to have none but the most friendly relations. Our weapons are for the oppressors of Ireland. Our blows shall be directed only against the power of England..."

native people were squeezed into an mercantile formula to benefit the victors.

A more apt comparison might be South Africa where, as in Ireland, the descendants of minority Protestant landowners came to regard their property and political rights as no less authentic – even more so – than those of displaced native people. Ironically, the rising of 1848 was led by a remarkable non-Catholic: William Smith O'Brien.

Let's zoom in for a moment on the Atkinson family's patron saint[1]:

O'Brien is a towering figure in the history of Irish nationalism not for what he accomplished (arguably very little), but for what he was willing to throw away (just about everything). He was a wealthy landowning Protestant, a member of British Parliament and of royal lineage.[2] That's

---

1   Elizabeth Atkinson's mother was Lucy O'Brien, a cousin of William Smith O'Brien, probably descended from an illustrious line dating to Sir Lucius O'Brien. James and Elizabeth named one of their sons for the nationalist hero. O'Brien Atkinson and his wife Mary had no children, but Colonel John Atkinson kept the tradition alive by naming one of his sons O'Brien. Today in Baltimore, Maryland, are the fourth and fifth generation O'Brien Atkinsons (the great-great and great-great-great grandson of the Colonel).

2   He was the second son of Sir Edward O'Brien, fourth Baronet of Dromoland Castle.

a three-for-three antithesis of what you would expect in a fighter for Catholic rights. O'Brien personally stood to gain nothing. This made him all the more beloved by Catholics, and detested by his ruling-class peers.

For many years in Parliament, O'Brien championed the lost cause of Catholic "emancipation," which by the 1840s was primarily an issue of land rights. He argued for non-violent political solutions, but gradually was radicalized and drawn to the militant Young Ireland movement. His advocacy for a Catholic "national guard" finally was too much.

In 1848 he led a symbolic non-violent march on a police station, which turned into something of a brawl. This was the chance authorities had been waiting for. Charged with "sedition", O'Brien was sentenced to be hanged, drawn and quartered – the customary form of execution for treason. But after 70,000 petition signatures, mostly from Catholics, the punishment was reduced to "transportation for life." He was exiled to remote islands off Tasmania.

Although eventually he was pardoned, O'Brien never returned to public life and was by most accounts a dispirited and broken man. He died in June, 1864, less than two years before the American Fenians would make their own march for Catholic advancement.

CONDITIONS IN 19TH CENTURY Ireland had eased considerably since 1649, but for Catholics the nation remained a kind of Jim Crow colony. The Act of Union in 1800 made Ireland and Scotland theoretical co-equals with Britain in a United Kingdom, but four-fifths of the Irish population had no meaningful part in it. Catholics had recently been granted the right to vote, but they themselves could not hold high office.

So-called "Catholic emancipation" became a cause not unlike the American civil rights movement – and equally attended with violence. Led by Daniel O'Connell, allied Protestant dissenters and sympathetic English politicians, Catholics won the right to send their own M. P.s to Parliament in 1829. (It is worth noting that Great Britain abolished slavery four years after granting political representation to Irish Catholics.) But for many Catholics even this concession smacked of bargaining with "The Thief" for piecemeal return of stolen treasure. There could be no gratefulness in the transaction.

(In light of this history, the reader is reminded that nationalist leader Michael Collins – after gaining a "free state" for most of Ireland in 1921 – was nevertheless assassinated as a traitor to the cause by radicalized members of his own coalition.)

So for those 150,000 Irish Catholic veterans of the Union

armies in 1865, and for their families, now comprising roughly two million Americans – immigrants all – the Old Sod was not the picturesque and sentimental homeland that we think of today. It was an island-prison. Subjugation of Catholic Irish by the "Saxon vampire" was a raw reality. Suspicion and hatred of all things British was the mother's milk of the Irish immigrant psychology.

(The reader may consult many fine, detailed histories of the Irish catastrophe. We include several titles in our bibliography.)

Writing in the 1950s, Churchill called Cromwell's invasion an "uncomplicated process of terror" and the great tragedy among English-speaking people around the world... "the lasting bane of relations. Across three hundred years the consequences of Cromwell's rule in Ireland... have baffled the skills and loyalties of successive generations (to heal them). Upon all of us there still lies the 'curse of Cromwell.'"

PART 3

"A man who... throws his whole soul into it."

One day in the summer of 1868 an "ingratiating" stranger appeared in Port Huron and immediately began "associating himself with the considerable number of Irish there."

Most likely the visitor posed as a salesman. He was a good one. Over the next several days, by calling on mill owners and store proprietors, he was able to make an "examination of storehouses, mills and barns, etc." He was searching for unassembled artillery pieces, or "concealed arms or boxes that might contain them."

No obvious weapons caches were found.[1] But amongst the Irish there was plenty of talk to enliven the agent's report and alarm his employers.

Some weeks earlier, the new Pinkerton agency in New York City received an assignment from the Secretary of War marked urgent: investigate the key "western" Fenian circles to ascertain when and where they plan to strike (again). Allan Pinkerton, of Presbyterian Scottish lineage, was a Fenian

---

1 Two years later, in May of 1870, the Michigan corps of Fenians would have 10,000 stand of arms secreted in barns and warehouses between Port Huron and Detroit.

specialist. Two years earlier he had personally done surveillance work for a British spymaster in Ottawa, and he had heard of the Atkinsons: the Catholic family with a Canadian background yet a British-sounding name.

Pinkerton – the first chief of military intelligence for Union armies during the war, and the first to create a "detective agency" – sometimes is credited with perfecting the technique of assuming a role. Today we call it undercover. And for this assignment Pinkerton chose his agents well. All were Irish and with the right word could pass as nationalists. But they were not descendants of native dispossessed majority Catholics. They were in fact Protestant "Orangemen" from Ulster, a stronghold of British domination in Ireland.

In other words, Pinkerton's spies were a personification of British rule the Fenians were sworn to destroy. This ensured that his detectives were reliable and keenly motivated in their work, and they could not be turned as double agents. It also added a quotient of personal hazard to the job.[1]

This element of risk makes it all the more remarkable that Pinkerton's man in Port Huron – who clearly was able to meet

---

1 In his report, Pinkerton complained that his men were not given "the time that a good detective needs to ingratiate (himself) ... and get on familiar terms with those upon whom (he) desires to operate."

and size up two of the Atkinson brothers in his perambulations around town – offered a somewhat charming appraisal.

Of the oldest brother, O'Brien (whom the agent referred to as "Colonel," his Fenian rank), Pinkerton said: "he is 27 or 28 years of age, five feet 10 inches in height, slim build, but muscular, walks straight and erect, clear complexion... dark hair inclined to curl, combed back of his ears, has fine, clear expression, dark hazel eyes, brown mustache."

William's profile was muscular too. Although the youngest of the three Fenian brothers, he was in 1867 elected "Head Centre" of the Port Huron circle. Pinkerton wrote: "he is about 25, five feet seven inches in height... slim built, but muscular, very straight, with long black curly hair, of which he is apparently very proud, and which he combs back of his ears, has fine expressive eyes, rather thin face, small dark mustache, dresses well, almost foppishly, but he apparently is a man who when he goes into any movement throws his whole soul into it."

Such detailed personal descriptions are rare for the time. In the complete Pinkerton report – encompassing not only Port Huron but Cleveland, Chicago and Detroit – only the Atkinson brothers are named.

O'Brien and William were said to be "men of a high order of intellect and ability, and reputed as honest and fair in their dealings... yet (they are) devoted Fenians. Captain (William)

Atkinson has been east attending the Fenian convention in New York city (sic), but has lately returned and apparently is busily engaged – though upon what could not be learned."

"Their time is about equally divided between Port Huron and Detroit. It is said neither of the brothers go into Canada.[1] Should a movement take place along the St. Clair River, from all I can learn it is possible the Atkinsons will be the leaders in it," Pinkerton said.

We can say with a good deal of confidence that Pinkerton's agent did not encounter John Atkinson, for his report would have taken up several more paragraphs. Newspaper accounts describe John as a man of oratorical gifts, political savvy and a "tall... commanding" physical stature, with a sharp ear for the perceived insult and a one-two kickboxing technique that he used to take down his adversaries.

Colonel John would become one of the most acclaimed trial lawyers of the late 19th century, but talked about as much for fisticuffs in various courtrooms as his Darrow-like summations (which were standing-room-only in Detroit).

---

1 This is probably untrue. William may already have been courting Katherine (Kate) M. Donnelly of Plympton, Canada. Documents of the time indicate the Atkinson brothers were doing business with Canadian firms across the river. More about this later.

Shouting distance

At the southernmost tip of Lake Huron where the American and Canadian shorelines come almost within shouting distance across the St. Clair River, one may discern an ideal launch point for invasion: Port Huron.

In good weather a dawn crossing in force to Sarnia, Ontario, would entail hardly more than strenuous rowing. And in winter, when the river freezes, a regiment could stroll the few thousand feet separating the United States from what was then British North America, defended by amateur militia and a thin line of the Queen's Own. Popcorn for hardened former Union soldiers.

In his analysis for the War Department, September 3, 1868, Pinkerton warned: "there is no evidence to lead to the impression that any movement on Canada (is) contemplated before the river freezes over, but it was very plainly intimated that after the river was frozen over there would be an invasion." (His forecast was off by roughly a year.)

Pinkerton added: "In this respect I would say... that it is not difficult at all to make a movement from along the river St. Clair over to Canada in the summer time, as the river can easily be crossed, either by steamers, scows, barges, or floats."[1]

The brothers Atkinson and other Fenian leaders in Michigan believed that once a fighting lodgement was secured near Sarnia, a large corps of second-echelon troops would be rushed by rail from Chicago – cavalry, artillery and thousands of men were promised. But this didn't worry Pinkerton. It seems cliché to say it now, but Chicago was easily the most corrupt of the Fenian circles.[2]

Pinkerton took the Chicago leg of the War Department assignment himself and summed up the situation there as follows:

1　The report continues at considerable length in descriptions of local wharves and potential river-crossing venues at "Avery's saw mill" two miles south of Port Huron, "Sturgeon's shingle mill" still further south, "Carlton's wharf", "Yankee street" and many small communities known only by the name of a mill owner, all the way to Marine City. These descriptions, including topographical details, numbers of barns, etc., were intended to provide landmarks for federal troops responding to a potential Fenian attack.

2　One outdoor rally or "picnic" of the Republican Fenian Club in Chicago on August 12, 1868, drew 50,000 people. This level of attendance was not unusual. Donations for "invasion funds" were coerced at these rallies.

"There is quite a large Fenian organization in Chicago, but it is very weak on account of lack of funds. The leaders appear to have drained their followers of nearly all their means … much dissension prevails among them (the Fenian rank and file). They would undoubtedly be willing to participate in any raid upon Canada, but they lack confidence in their leaders…."

Pinkerton sounded almost sympathetic. "They (rank and file Fenians) would hesitate to follow their leaders into any active movement without they were better assured (sic) than they are now that their leaders would be more sincere with them than they have hitherto been. I am safe I think in saying that so far as Chicago is concerned there is very little danger of a movement of Fenians from that city."

Events would prove Pinkerton right.

Sixty miles south of Port Huron, at the western end of Lake Erie, another strategic gem is Detroit. Well served by shipping and rail lines, and home to a sizeable Irish immigrant population, Detroit could accommodate the expected thousands of troops arriving incognito from around the Midwest in the days prior to invasion, cloistered in hotels and friendly homes, all waiting for H-hour.

Port Huron and Detroit were considered critical elements of Fenian plans in 1866 and again in 1870.

For both invasions the tactical objectives of this western flank were the same: engage and rout Canadian military units at Sarnia, Windsor, Amherstburg and points east through sparsely inhabited farmland along the northern shore of Lake Erie. Commandeer locomotives of the Great Western railway and hasten eastward, neutralizing stations on the way, to converge on a march toward Ottawa (1866) or join O'Neill's forces in Quebec (1870).

The strategic objective: divert Canadian units away from the main crossing on the New York-Vermont border.

The prize: capture and consolidation of Ontario (1866) or the St. Lawrence Seaway (1870), Canada's commercial lifeline.

If the Fenians could seize and occupy a swath of Queen Victoria's territory, perhaps even an entire province, Irish Catholics would for the first time in centuries have real cards to play. They could declare a new Irish Republic (already home to thousands of immigrant Irish who theoretically would rise up to welcome their liberators). Or they could use Ontario as a base of operations against British shipping. They might even barter the province for Catholic "emancipation" in Ireland.

In the bargain, a successful invasion would probably force war between America and Britain. Relations already were tense. Ireland could only benefit.

Now... at this point the reader will be forgiven a moment of incredulity.

"Declare a new Irish Republic in Ontario"? Or trade part of Canada for Irish Catholic "emancipation?"

For most Americans who have never heard of the Fenian movement, the details can come across – all these comfortable years later – like a John Belushi movie with a cast of zany characters and a wild premise.

But that perception is a trick of time. Nobody was kidding in the late 1860s. Although they'd been stopped once before, in 1866, the Fenians had quite a few reasons to think they could still bring off a conquest of British territory in 1870 – or at least enough of it to get everyone's attention.

Not least of these reasons was a tacit "assurance" from the government.

Which brings us to Andrew Johnson. Today he is dimly remembered as Lincoln's successor and the only president who shares a peculiar niche with Bill Clinton – Johnson was impeached by the House in 1868.[1] Johnson's case was entirely politically-based over Reconstruction policy. In fact, the basis for charges, the Tenure of Office Act, was later declared unconstitutional. The cantankerous Tennessean – an unapologetic white supremacist – eventually was acquitted in the Senate by one vote.

---

1   Richard Nixon resigned in 1974 before the House formally voted on impeachment.

What's important to our story is that the only thing Johnson and his Congressional tormentors did agree on was Great Britain: which had not endeared itself to the Union during the Civil War. This was where Fenian passions and the government's interests perfectly aligned, and a dance of political opportunism ensued.

"Private assurances..."

Some historians have labeled the Fenians' large ambitions not only naïve but irrational. Abstruse is a favorite word. You decide. Let's take a look at the bitter street-fight that was national politics and international affairs after the Civil War.

Relations with Britain were never chummy during the 19th century (i.e., the War of 1812 and innumerable border squabbles regarding Canada), but they reached a new nadir in the Civil War. The British never openly endorsed the Confederacy, but they recognized the government in Richmond as a "belligerent power" – infuriating Washington. All through the war Lincoln was under pressure to abrogate trade treaties in retaliation. But far more serious was Britain's not-so-subtle military aid to the rebels.

During the war several vessels (including a couple of ironclads) were built in English shipyards under lucrative contracts from the Confederacy. One raider in particular, "The Alabama," had been a scourge to Union shipping.

In less than two years, the *CSS Alabama* captured, sank or burned 68 Union-chartered ships before finally being cornered and sunk by the *USS Kearsarge* off the coast of France in 1864.

As early as 1862, when the war's outcome was still in doubt, Washington issued angry diplomatic protests. And the

British eventually quarantined those two ironclads. But with victory in 1865 came a chorus of denunciation and demands for reparations. Congress and the Johnson administration were quoting figures upward of $2 billion for commercial losses to "The Alabama." London stalled, hoping the matter would fade. It didn't. The "Alabama Claims" became a national grindstone. At one point Senator Charles Sumner suggested Britain had only two choices – pay up or cede all of Canada as compensation.

(It's fascinating to note that the life span of the "Alabama Claims," which were finally resolved by a treaty in 1871, almost exactly corresponds to that period when Fenian activities were tolerated by the government.)

Canada wasn't on Washington's A-list either.

During the war Confederate guerillas used British North America as a "neutral" safe-haven from which to harass Union border towns. One spectacular raid into St. Albans, Vermont, still had northern editorialists fulminating. As late as March of 1866 the *Port Huron Press* said: "There is a natural feeling that Canada... which so largely sympathized with the rebel raiders... should have a taste of the state of affairs on this side of the border in the last year of our war."

Keep in mind: this was a time when Americans considered "the provinces" little more than a holdover from the British colonial enterprise – still thinly populated, particularly in western regions, despite decades of attempts by the British to entice settlement. Annexation or (the euphemistic term) "absorption" of Canadian territory was not only thinkable, many believed it was inevitable. "Continentalists" didn't confine their vision of America's manifest destiny to the west alone. Ontario seemed a perfect fit, for starters.

Unroll a map. With your eye trace a line along the "pine belt" from Maine to Minnesota. Jefferson once famously declared that annexation of Ontario would be a "mere matter of marching."

Forty years later, the Fenians thought so too.

Meanwhile, politicians in northern states ardently courted the Irish... praising their wartime heroism to the heavens. For more than a generation, Democrats had owned (literally) the Irish vote. But now with a Republican president rumored to be "sympathetic" to the Fenian cause, Irish veterans were no longer a lock. As a fractured Republican party and Democrats fought desperately for control of Congress in 1866 and again in 1868, no one seeking office wanted to be on the wrong side of the "Fenian question."

Typical was the political environment in Port Huron:

Pinkerton's agent reported that "heavy bids are being offered for the Fenian vote... and Fenian movements are winked at by prominent politicians to secure the Irish vote."

For an immigrant population of Catholic Irish that before the war had been held somewhere between suspicion and contempt, these were heady times. Then as now, politicians were quick to define the language of electability. In speeches from the Senate floor to the campaign stump, Democrats (attempting to hold their traditional base of support) and Republicans (attempting to steal it) competed for who could revile the British – loudest and longest.

Fenian membership spiked to perhaps 80,000 men nationwide, and fund-raising reached a crescendo. At an Irish National Fair in Chicago, for example, handfuls of sacred "Irish turf" were sold in envelopes for 25-cents each. Thousands of Fenian "War Bonds" were issued (to be redeemed by the anticipated New Nation). One reported meeting at Chicago's Metropolitan Hall saw 1,000 former Union cavalry officers pledging to the fight 37,000 men from across Illinois... all waiting for the word.

It seemed to many Fenian leaders that History was presenting them with a unique opportunity – but one with an expiration date. They had an "army" ready to strike, but soon these men would return home and take up civilian life. They had public sentiment, too, but for how much longer? Precisely at this moment a split developed within the leadership.

President O'Mahony, the old revolutionary, hesitated. Still in despair over the shocking and swift demise of the

IRB only months earlier, O'Mahony worried that Fenian circles – by now more than 600 – were also infiltrated with spies (they were). He'd been focused for so long on action in Ireland, the Canada scheme seemed a futile gesture. More accustomed to speech-making and plotting and defeatism in Ireland, O'Mahony found himself riding the expectations of a brotherhood of a far different character: Americanized, self-confident, tired of talking, anxious for action. Gradually he was pushed aside.

And so at their convention in 1866, about the same time as O'Brien Atkinson's first Fenian get-together in Port Huron, a majority radical faction of the Brotherhood openly declared itself "at war with the oligarchy of Great Britain." Most newspaper readers, including members of the Johnson administration, were little concerned by these florid developments. But the British, who well understood the hatred of Catholic Irish immigrants, took them seriously.[1]

Perhaps the catalytic event is one that historians usually brush over.

---

1 That year a member of the House of Commons declared the Fenians "a new Irish nation on the other side of the Atlantic, recast in the mould of Democracy, waiting for an opportunity to strike a blow at the heart of the Empire."

In spring of 1866, as negotiations with Britain over "The Alabama Claims" were going nowhere, Johnson and Secretary of State William Seward decided it would be useful to invite a Fenian leader or two to the Executive Mansion[1] for a widely-publicized chat. As reported in the *Detroit Free Press* on April 9, 1866, Bernard Killian, the top aide to O'Mahony, briefed the two leaders on Fenian intentions... and received what he bragged were their "private assurances of support."

Should the Fenians successfully invade Canada – success defined as being able to secure and *defend* a significant chunk of territory – Johnson, according to Killian, promised to "recognize accomplished facts."

Imagine.

Chances are good that Killian, although he was obviously misled, nevertheless was reporting accurately. A telling diary entry from Secretary of the Navy Gideon Welles, published in 1960, bitterly complained that "Seward and (Secretary of War) Stanton are very chary about disturbing the Fenians... and I do not care to travel out of the line of duty" to cross the administration's hands-off policy.

A letter to Ottawa from a Washington-based Canadian diplomat dovetails with this impression: "I tell you now there is a perfect understanding between Seward and two Fenian

---

1   Only decades later was it called The White House.

chiefs."[2]

News of the Killian meeting electrified the Fenians. They were convinced the federal government would not interfere. It would have been difficult for them to conclude otherwise. At this point Fenian leaders were allowed (even encouraged) to purchase arms and ammunition from government arsenals. Their stockpiles eventually totaled 10,000 rifles and muskets and 2.5 million rounds of ammunition (but significantly, no artillery.)[3] Fenian brigades were permitted to drill, conduct war exercises and parade publicly in large cities, all without a contrary word from federal officials.

---

2   This letter and other private "warnings" were found in the papers of John A. McDonald, who would become Canada's first Prime Minister.

3   The Fenians, of course, recognized that the government was off-loading some of its surplus weaponry (left over from the war) at a profit. And they understood Seward was engaged in a double-game, using Fenian threats against Canada to pressure the British for Civil War damages.   But these equations seemed fair enough, as long as they advanced the Fenian agenda.

Sarnia braces for invasion

In the wild months leading up to the first attack in 1866, the Fenians made no secret of their preparations. Meetings were open to the public. Reporters telegraphed breathless updates and rumors, which editors around the country generally printed as is. In Port Huron, with the Canadian border just a casual glance away, the weekly *Port Huron Press* and *St. Clair Republican* gave front-page coverage to the "March Scare":

March 7, 1866:

"An immense Fenian meeting was held in Jones' Wood,
near New York ... O'Mahony and others in his faction promised
the landing of an army in Ireland within six weeks."
[NOTE: the larger rival faction, led by William Roberts,
had already decided on Canada.]

March 14:

"It is estimated at Fenian headquarters in New York that
nearly 1,000,000 (that's not a typo: one million) men are ready to
move for the liberation of Ireland." [NOTE: This was a typical
overstatement designed to frighten the British, which it did, and
bolster the courage of Fenians.]

Also in the March 14, Port Huron Press:

"Fenian Scare"

"Last Wednesday night the (Canadian) militia were called out
to guard against an apprehended raid by the Fenians.
At Montreal the militia were under arms and a report prevailed
that 10,000 Fenians had seized Navy Island. [NOTE: Both
reports were completely untrue.] A cabinet meeting at Ottawa last
week determined to call out 10,000 volunteers for protection
of the Canadian frontier."

March 21:

"The Fenian excitement continues in Canada and troops are
being continually forwarded to the frontier.
A statement is published that the Chicago Fenians have
agreed to furnish three regiments of infantry, two batteries
of artillery and a naval brigade of 1,000 men, 8,000 stand
of arms and $600,000 in money."

Like other Irish around the country, in Port Huron the Atkinsons no doubt crowded the telegraph and editorial offices for updates. But the trio of Fenian brothers did not play an active role in this early episode. O'Brien was preoccupied with his new legal and political career (he had also opened an insurance business). John had only recently mustered out. And William was still in Texas with the 3rd Michigan.

Across the river in Sarnia, however, the population was "gripped by military fever."

Canadian authorities expected brigades, divisions... armies of Fenians at their border virtually any hour. But where? Buffalo and Vermont were obvious crossing points; Port Huron and Detroit too. As many as 4,000 nervous British regulars began arriving in the Sarnia area by train and were met at the station by cheering crowds and brass bands.[1] Sentries were posted along the St. Clair River and locomotives in Sarnia were kept under steam for evacuation.

But there was a madcap aspect to all this. As amateur local militia units mobilized, the preparations were nothing short of picturesque:

"In nearby Mooretown, for example, "farmers grew tired of marching and they formed a cavalry unit made up of their heavy draft horses and armed with scythes, pitchforks and the odd pike pole."

---

1   From "a History of Sarnia to 1900."

"Once, when they came on a charge near one of the sentry posts, the sentries sent out an alarm that Fenians were attacking, which caused much consternation and the eventual court marshal (sic) of the sentries."[2]

Several memoirs mention townspeople in Sarnia looking anxiously across the river and observing Fenian formations in close-order drill. One "eyewitness" counted 700 Fenians massing outside Port Huron. (These formations were more likely U. S. Army regulars stationed at Fort Gratiot.) Another man claimed to have seen small groups of Fenians crossing the river ice near Froomfield.

But much as the reader (and narrator) might wish to enjoy the spectacle of scythe- and pitchfork-wielding Lambton County farmers, mounted on Belgian draught horses, charging into a brigade of green-clad Fenians expecting a walkover in western Ontario, this was not to be. The overhyped Fenian crossing occurred not at Sarnia but Buffalo and nearby points along the Niagara River.

The invasion of 1866 is not our main topic, so we'll summarize: it was a fiasco.

Fenian commander-in-chief General Thomas Sweeny, on leave from the United States Army, envisioned a "thousand

---

2   From "a History of Sarnia to 1900."

mile front" with nearly simultaneous attacks at five different points in Ontario and Quebec, including an amphibious assault from Cleveland across Lake Erie – all converging to a unified advance toward Montreal and Ottawa. The logistics would have been dicey even if commanders were using GPS and cell phones instead of telegraphs and couriers on horseback.

As many as 2,000 various Fenian units (comprising perhaps 50,000 men) were supposed to coordinate their clandestine departures and arrive (quietly) at a dozen staging areas in Michigan, Ohio, New York and Vermont – on precise timetables – from as far away as New Orleans, St. Louis and points west. The rail transportation grid of 1866 was hopelessly outmatched. Hundreds of units missed their connections, were delayed, misinterpreted their instructions or simply never departed.[1] Chicago's vaunted Fenian cavalry, slated for a drive into Windsor from Detroit, was a stupendous no-show (which Allan Pinkerton would have predicted).

---

1   One often-overlooked reason for this fiasco: in mid-19th century America there were no regional time-zones. More than 300 different cities set their own standards based on "local sun time." This meant that travelers needed to re-set their timepieces – on average – every 12 miles. One simple re-calculation error could easily compound into a missed train connection somewhere.

It wasn't until 1883 when Congress mandated the four standard time zones we know today. The primary reason: catastrophic railroad accidents from misread schedules and timetables.

But from this chaos one genuine star did emerge: a flamboyant soldier-of-fortune named John O'Neill.

O'Neill takes command

John O'Neill was born in 1834 six weeks after his father died of plague, then he was handed off to relatives when his mother left for America. Twenty-three years later, O'Neill found his own way across the Atlantic – looking not for his mother but for adventure and a fight. In 1857 he joined the regular United States Army for expeditions into Utah and Indian country. Later he spent time in California among the Irish immigrants. And when the Civil War promised fame, he transferred to the 5th Indiana Cavalry.

O'Neill apparently was born to the uniform. Different accounts tell of a "fine looking man" at least six feet tall with a "rich sonorous voice" and an "undoubted military bearing." (Almost the same vocabulary was used to describe Colonel John Atkinson, who became closely associated with O'Neill, as we will see.)

For all practical purposes, however, O'Neill's aspirations for glory ended in 1863 at the siege of Knoxville, where he was "severely" injured. Details are scarce, but the injury prevented him from riding a horse: a prerequisite for field command. He transferred out of the cavalry and briefly led a "colored" infantry regiment, rising to colonel, but O'Neill would never have a Chickamauga to point to... as the Atkinsons could. Early in 1864 he resigned his officer's commission, took a job as a land claims agent and settled in Nashville, Tennessee. Here two pivotal events occurred.

First: he met then-Senator Andrew Johnson, who was military governor for the state. (This will become crucially important a few pages further.)

Second: O'Neill met and fell in love with the Fenian movement, which was then sweeping through Union ranks and across northern American cities. When a new circle was established in Union-occupied Nashville, O'Neill was made regimental commander. From that time forward, striking a blow at the "Saxon vampire" became his life's work. He could never have imagined how quickly and soon he would be given the reins of national leadership – simply by showing up.

On the 29ᵗʰ of May, 1866, with Sweeny's invasion plan already in pieces, O'Neill arrived in Cleveland with less than 200 men from the 13ᵗʰ Fenian Tennessee regiment. There were no boats for the Lake Erie crossing, and no orders from Sweeny in the East. Scattered units, hundreds of men who had arrived days earlier, now were holed up in warehouses along the waterfront. And the regional commander, General W. F. Lynch, was "unaccountably" absent.[1]

It turned out that O'Neill was the ranking officer. He took command.

Now a brevet General, O'Neill and his ad hoc ensemble of troops made their way to the rendezvous point in Buffalo by May 31ˢᵗ. There a courier presented Sweeny's handwritten orders, now several days old, calling for an assault the following day. And so in the pre-dawn hours of June 1ˢᵗ, commanding roughly 2,000 Fenians aboard tugboats and barges, O'Neill crossed the Niagara. He landed virtually unopposed.

Canadian authorities – despite repeated warnings from their consulate and months of Fenian braggadocio, even despite an incompetent Fenian raid at Campobello Island

---

1 Defections from command at crucial moments was a continuous problem for the Fenians, as we shall see again in 1870.

weeks earlier[1] – simply couldn't believe an "Irish army" had materialized on their soil. "Those damned Fenians"[2] had actually done it.

The Johnson administration seemed indifferent. No orders to intervene were forthcoming from Washington. Federal marshals and the handful of U. S. troops stationed along the American-Canadian border were little more than onlookers. Buffalo citizens, as the morning broke, lined the river hoping to catch a glimpse of combat.

O'Neill's men secured a canal (for delivery of supplies and reinforcements), cut telegraph lines, marched southwest

---

1   In mid-April, emboldened by his conference with Johnson, Killian led a local Fenian brigade intending to occupy Campobello Island – later a favorite retreat of President Franklin D. Roosevelt, but then an undefended lighthouse station in Passamaquoddy Bay between Maine and New Brunswick. Provenance of the island had never been formally established. Great Britain and America claimed it. Killian's goal was to exchange gunfire with British troops and stoke up the Anglo-American crisis.

Killian never made the crossing. He and several hundred Fenians loitered in Eastport, Maine, believing that they had plenty of time, casually chartering vessels and awaiting reinforcements. Instead they were met by a detachment of federal troops with orders to disperse.

2   This was a recent offhand comment by a Canadian newspaperman – half joking, but half not – while discussing source-material for this narrative.

and, without firing a shot, "captured" the sleeping town of Fort Erie. Hours later, at nearby Ridgeway, they met and routed a sizeable brigade of militia hastily dispatched from Toronto. Nearly a dozen Canadians were killed (and a like number of Fenians).[3] Ridgeway instantly became a kind of Bunker Hill for Canadians, and today is considered a seminal event in national history. O'Neill's two-day adventure united the eastern provinces as only an invasion – with casualties – can.

Within a year of Ridgeway, a Canadian Confederation had been created, largely for self-defense against the Fenians.[4]

But we promised to summarize.

The short of it is that O'Neill's assault forces – out of ammunition, desperately needing reinforcement, and with

---

3 No two sources agree on casualty figures at Ridgeway, which likely were exaggerated by both sides for political purposes.

4 In the 1860s more than 95% of the population of British North America lived in the five eastern colonies. Western regions were practically untouched by settlement. (This, again, was what fueled the persistent American notion of territorial absorption.) By the time of William Atkinson's "slap at Canada" in 1870, these five eastern provinces could dispatch their own full-time professionals rather than rely on British garrisons.

An interesting sidebar to Canadian Confederation: there were 13 so-called colonies in British North America. Ten provinces eventually joined the confederation. Three others remain "territories." Not until 1949 did Newfoundland join.

British regulars now bearing down on them – were cut off and left to wither. On his own initiative the commander of a U. S. Navy frigate, the *Michigan*, intercepted 700 more troops attempting to cross. Marshals gathered their wits and began making mass arrests in Buffalo. A smaller incursion from Vermont also was stopped. Sweeny, too, was arrested and the perplexed Fenians went sullenly into custody.

Finally on June 5 – four days later – President Johnson issued a laconic proclamation reminding "all Americans" of the 1818 Neutrality Act. General O'Neill was already in custody, with no choice but to retreat and surrender to authorities.

The governments in Ottawa and London were livid… apoplectic. A number of Fenian stragglers were captured during O'Neill's chaotic scramble back across the Niagara, and Canadians promptly announced they would all be hanged. General George Meade, still in the army and now a regional commander, was finally sent to "cool out" the situation. As he had at Gettysburg, Meade proved an adept improviser.

With thousands of late-arriving Fenians now in local jails, or crammed onto barges on the Niagara River under the guns of U. S. Navy cutters, Meade offered a free train ticket home to rank-and-file soldiers who would sign an oath – basically promising not to bother Canada again. Virtually all the Irish signed and went home.

Fenian officers, including O'Neill, were held for trial

in Buffalo. At which point we meet another famous name in the cavalcade. One of the city's top lawyers in 1866 was future president Grover Cleveland. He seized on the headline opportunity to act as counsel for the Fenians – pro bono. But it was mostly for show. A resolution by Congress in July urged that all prosecutions (for violating the Neutrality Act) be dropped. The Irish vote still mattered.

O'Neill and other Fenians – considered hoodlums by the Canadians and British, but now seen by many Americans as quixotic rascals – were freed to wild celebrations in Buffalo.

As for those two dozen Fenian prisoners still in Canada, no such luck. They were tried in Toronto under British death-penalty statutes dating to the Mackenzie revolt in 1837, which made it a capital crime to enter Canada for the purpose of inciting insurrection. (One of the Fenians' expressed aims was for all Irish Catholic Canadians to join their cause.) The prisoners were convicted, but under pressure from Washington their sentences were commuted to 20 years of hard labor. None served more than a few years – the last prisoner from the 1866 invasion was released in 1872.

Meanwhile, the process of resolving those "Alabama Claims" ground on.

(Above) British officers in Ireland: By the end of the American Civil War, Ireland had been a militarily-occupied British colony for more than two centuries, with dispossessed native Gaels (Catholic Irish) relegated to apartheid status. Although nominally part of the United Kingdom (with Scotland and Britain) since 1800, the island was in reality a vast British plantation under direct rule from London, administered by Protestant landlords and a pro-Union Irish Parliament.

 Beginning with the Elizabethan conquest in the late 16th century – as they would do in India and elsewhere during Britain's long reign as the world's pre-eminent power – the British installed Penal Laws, discriminatory tax codes and import-export policies which systematically reduced Ireland's economic viability to that of a dependent agrarian state. (Similar mercantile policies are what later provoked revolution by British colonists in America.)

 Even in the depths of a worldwide potato blight, 1845-46, when the United States and other European countries were turning to alternative food crops, Irish tenant-farmers were required to export healthy corn, wheat and oats to England, leaving only a diseased potato crop for personal sustenance. One million Irish died or emigrated on so-called "coffin ships." Historians have argued the Great Famine was in many respects an artificial catastrophe, engineered by landlords using complicit government policies to depopulate and clear agricultural land.

 This was the backdrop of the doomed 1848 Young Ireland rising. Although it was quickly crushed, a handful of surviving leaders would resurface a generation later in America as the Fenian vanguard.

Plate 1

Oliver Cromwell, 1599 – 1658:

By far the most hated figure in Irish Catholic history, Cromwell came to power as commander of Parliamentarian forces during the English Civil Wars of the 1640s – he signed Charles I's death warrant in 1649. A Puritan zealot, Cromwell then launched the rapacious "re-conquest" of Ireland in which thousands of Catholic landowners, farmers and peasants were ethnically cleansed, their children sold into slavery and Catholic lands awarded to Protestant investors.

When royalists returned to power in England in 1860, Cromwell's corpse was exhumed and beheaded. But the damage in Ireland could not be undone. Cromwell's divisive legacy persists to this day.

Plate 2

Ireland's own version of "9/11" was the Massacre of Drogheda *(above left)*,
September 11, 1649, when Cromwell's forces overwhelmed a small Catholic
garrison and – as a warning to other towns still resisting – slaughtered 3,000
unarmed and fleeing clergy and civilians. Cromwell then marched on to
Wexford, killing 2,000 more civilians. England's maverick Charles I *(above
right)* had married a French Catholic princess, claimed the "divine right of
kings" and engaged in a bitter 25-year power struggle with Parliament –
which culminated in his beheading *(below)*.

Plate 3

Period cartoon of Queen Victoria confronted by "Ireland in chains."

Plate 4

EVICTION SCENE. 1767. W.L.

Forced eviction was a tactic that absentee land owners used to clear their holdings of Irish "squatters" for more profitable tillage, cattle or sheep. Between 1846 and 1854, as landlords "screwed up" the rents, an estimated 150,000 tenant-farmer families (virtually all Catholic) lost their homes, leaving them no choice but to emigrate or subsist on "government relief" at so-called workhouses. Evictions *(above)* were carried out by hired "bailiffs" and "crowbar brigades" – accompanied by police – who immediately leveled the vacated dwelling.

The plight of Irish tenants during the Famine outraged even some sympathizers in British government. Lord Lieutenant of Ireland, the Earl of Clarendon, bitterly complained of inaction by Parliament as tantamount to a "policy of extermination." Relief programs were token efforts at best, and administration was miserly. One example was the Gregory Clause – part of the 1847 Irish Poor Law – which specified that tenants who owned more than a quarter-acre of land, regardless of other circumstances, did not qualify for assistance. As a result, thousands of starving Irish families were refused help. Meanwhile, landlords used the quarter-acre technicality as a means to coerce surrender of their homes by marginalized Irish who were desperate to qualify for aid.

Plate 5

Pictured *(above)* is an evicted Irish family in County Donegal, 1887: by the late 19th century, when much of Europe was at peace and relatively prosperous, diaries and letters show visitors to Ireland were appalled by still-medieval living conditions amongst the Catholic peasantry.

(Left) "Freedom to Ireland," a *Currier & Ives* lithograph, circa 1866.

Plate 6

Then as ever, monied interests cut a large swathe in government and
landlords were generally given a free hand in Ireland, even when evictions
led to deaths from exposure or starvation. At root, racism played a role in
British perceptions and thus British policies. Evicted Irish who accepted
(pitiable) government assistance were depicted in period English cartoons
(above left) as ape-like, obese, lazy, violent... "the working man's burden."
British Home Secretary, Sir George Grey, scoffed at the notion that "house-
destroying landlords" should be prosecuted. It was, after all, their property.
Parliament in fact enacted a new law reducing required eviction notice to
48 hours. The same law made it a misdemeanor to demolish a dwelling
with tenants still inside. In what seems a macabre gesture, evictions were
prohibited only on Christmas day and Good Friday.

(Above right) Sir Charles Trevelyan (1807-86), assistant secretary at the
treasury, became the face of British indifference during The Famine.
Although charged with overseeing government relief, Trevelyan publicly
declared famine was a useful "mechanism for reducing surplus population"
and a "judgement (sic) of God... to teach the Irish a lesson." He was
knighted for his (largely indiscernible) services during the crisis.

Plate 7

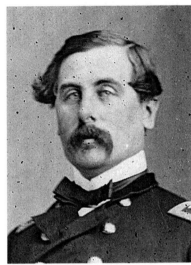

(Above left) Young Ireland leader William Smith O'Brien, 1803–1864, a distant relative of the Atkinsons. Although himself a wealthy Protestant of noble lineage, as a matter of conscience W. S. O'Brien championed "emancipation" and land reform for Catholics. Cherished by Irish Catholics, he was in equal measure despised as a traitor to his class by ruling Protestant peers. In 1849 O'Brien was convicted of high treason and banished to the British penal colony in Tasmania. Pardoned a decade later, he never returned to public life and died two years before the first Fenian invasion.

(Above right) Thomas Francis Meagher (1796-1874), who raised and commanded the Fighting 69th Irish Brigade at Second Bull Run, Antietam and Fredericksburg. Born in Waterford, Ireland, Meagher (with O'Mahony, D'Arcy McGee and William Smith O'Brien) was a leader of the short-lived 1848 Young Ireland revolt. Captured by the British and originally condemned to death, he was banished for life to Tasmania. Meagher escaped Tasmania in 1852 and made his way to New York City.

Plate 8

(Left) Designed in France and brought back to Ireland by nationalist leader Thomas Meagher in 1848, the Irish Tricolor symbolized the generous (some would say naïve) ideals of the Young Ireland movement. It is equal parts green, white and orange – green for native Catholic Irish, orange for landholding English (Anglicans) and Scots (Presbyterian), and white for reconciliation and equality. Inspired by political revolutions across Europe in 1848, most notably the overthrow of monarchy in France, Meagher and William Smith O'Brien believed nonviolent "moral force" could bring land reform and Irish "independence" from Britain. When an O'Brien-led march on a police station turned into a brick-throwing brawl, British authorities seized the opportunity to shut down the entire movement and arrest its leaders. The Tricolor was adopted in 1922 by the new Irish Free State as its national flag.

Meagher *(standing center)* and O'Brien *(seated)* under guard at Kilmainham Gaol, Dublin, prior to their deportation to Van Diemen's Land (Tasmania), Australia.

Plate 9

A TERRIBLE RECORD.

ERIN—In forty years I have lost, through the operation of no natural law, more than Three Millions of my Sons and Daughters, and they, the Young and the Strong, leaving behind the Old and the Infirm to weep and to die   Where is this to end ?

Supplement to the *Weekly Freeman,* July 2, 1881, entitled 'A Terrible Record':
"ERIN – In forty years I have lost, through the operation of no natural law, more than Three Millions of my Sons and Daughters, and they, the Young and the Strong, leaving behind the Old and Infirm to weep and die. Where is this to end?"

The controversial Act of Union in 1800 formally annexed Ireland as part of the United Kingdom. Executive power was exercised by a Lord Lieutenant of Ireland and Chief Secretary for Ireland, both appointed by London. Ireland did have representation in the British parliament, but Irish MPs were overwhelmingly Protestant landowners.

Mass evictions, unemployment (up to 75%) and local famines were a constant of life for the Catholic Irish majority – what Gladstone would later call "untold abominations." Between 1801 and 1845 no fewer than 114 commissions and 61 special committees were launched to investigate the "Irish problem." As one historian noted, "without exception their findings prophesied disaster." Many Catholic peasants met each new day on the brink of starvation "with a standard of living unbelievably low."

As alluded to in this poster, The Great Famine (1845-48) took no one by surprise – not government officials, not landowners (many of whom welcomed the prospect of having their lands "cleared") and certainly not Catholic peasants. More than one million Irish died outright; another million fled via emigration, reducing the island's native population by 25%.

Plate 10

After losing 13 of their prize colonies in the American Revolution, the British desperately sought settlers for their thinly-populated remaining Canadian possessions – collectively called British North America. Ocean-going fares to Halifax and Quebec *(above)* were heavily subsidized (and thus far less expensive than to New York or Boston). For this reason, many impoverished Irish families chose the "Canada route," then migrated to ports of entry at Buffalo and Port Huron for greater opportunity in the United States.

Arriving immigrant ships were required to stop for medical inspections at Grosse Île, sometimes called Canada's Ellis Island. But so overwhelming was the tide of Irish immigration during the Potato Famine, dozens of waiting ships languished while those on board coped with dwindling food and outbreaks of disease. On May 31, 1847, for example, some 40 vessels, with more than 13,000 emigrants, extended two miles down the St. Lawrence Seaway – another 45,000 immigrants were at sea and expected soon.

Plate 11

For Irish immigrants fleeing the Famine, death at the gateway to a new life
was common. This memorial at Grosse-Île, Quebec was erected in 1909
to commemorate thousands of shipboard victims of typhus – 5,000 in 1849
alone.

Shipping was not regulated in the 19th century and most Irish
sailed in vessels built to carry bulk goods, not people. Dank, cramped
lower decks were incubators for typhus, dysentery and communicable
disease. Conditions were worst aboard vessels contracted by landlords who
subsidized passage (to be rid of squatters). Corrupt quartermasters often
shorted supplies. Drinking water and provisions quickly ran out. Even
routine delays at sea (from storms or becalmed waters), or slow processing
at an arrival port (see the previous page), were life-threatening.

Outside of Ireland itself, burial grounds at Grosse-Île hold the greatest
number of Famine victims.

Plate 12

PART 4

"I gave you five full days"

The reader is asked – once again – to make sure those 1860s-era goggles are properly adjusted.

Seen today, O'Neill's 1866 invasion of Canada on rental barges without benefit of artillery, cavalry or naval support seems near-delusional. But for many Americans at the time (and not just the Irish), it had an electrifying effect. Public sentiment against Canada and her arrogant overlords in London was strong. Editorials reflect a smirking satisfaction in the Brits having had their noses bloodied by passionate if misguided Irish patriots. Ridgeway elevated O'Neill – the "man of action" – to legendary status.

That summer, O'Neill toured the nation to gauge support for a renewed attempt, attracting huge crowds and the usual complement of pandering politicians. At a mass rally in Chicago in August of 1866, none other than Speaker of the House Schuyler Colfax made his sympathies known: "I confess," he told the Irish audience, "that I was humiliated when our army was sent to do the dirty work of spies and detectives against the Fenians."[1]

Such elliptical statements of government support were (again) seized upon by the Fenians.

Over the next two years, O'Neill's ascendancy within the Fenian Brotherhood was comprehensive. O'Mahony was jettisoned. He helped to organize another rising in Ireland in 1867 – also a failure – and died in a New York tenement, impoverished and forgotten, 10 years later. Sweeny simply returned to the U. S. Army and retired in 1870. Killian, disgraced by Campobello, drifted back to his New York City law practice.

William Roberts, who had led the Fenian faction supporting the "Canada scheme," eventually relinquished the presidency to O'Neill in 1867, who now became arguably the most visible and influential Irish figure in the United States.[2]

Such was O'Neill's star power that in the spring of 1868 he was granted a private meeting with President Johnson, ostensibly to petition for the return of personal weapons seized by federal marshals in Buffalo. As we mentioned

---

1 Taken from reports in sessional papers of Canadian Parliament, 1872.

2 While Pinkerton agents were gathering intelligence in Port Huron, Detroit and Cleveland, in May of 1868, a Fenian regiment marched down Chicago's Wabash Avenue for O'Neill's personal review.

earlier, O'Neill and Johnson knew each other: both were Tennesseans. Before he became Lincoln's Vice President in 1864, Johnson was a Senator (the only Southern senator to stand with the Union) and the military governor in Nashville. O'Neill convalesced from his 1863 injury in Nashville and settled there after the war.

The meeting began cordially enough...

As to what transpired between these men we are indebted to the presence of a spy. One of O'Neill's trusted Fenian aides was an officer he had served with during the war – Major Henri le Caron, real name Thomas Miller Beach, who claimed French ancestry but was in fact a British-born raconteur. Le Caron (Beach) followed O'Neill into the Fenian movement but soon thought better of it and, rather than simply resign, turned informer for Scotland Yard and Canadian intelligence chief Gilbert McMicken. O'Neill never suspected.

In his entertaining memoir, Beach recalled that Johnson and O'Neill were engaged in good-natured banter when suddenly the Fenian general put the question – "why, sir, did you betray us by intervening at Ridgeway?"

Johnson's angry response floored O'Neill and Beach: "I gave you five full days before issuing that proclamation. What in God's name do you people want? If you could not get there in five days, by God, you could never get there."

However incredible this statement may seem, coming

from a sitting president in the Executive Mansion, it rang true. The Fenians' failure in 1866 was not due to government intervention – which came days later – but primarily to their own woeful logistics. They'd had no artillery or cavalry to press home the attack, no organized flotilla to bring across sufficient troops. Nor sufficient troops to begin with. Not even good maps.

In a sense, the government had only rescued the Fenians from themselves.

O'Neill presumably took this dressing-down at face value, consoling himself that he had not been the author of the 1866 fiasco. Next time would be different.

A few months later at the annual Fenian convention in Philadelphia – to thunderous applause – O'Neill unveiled his new plan for invasion in the spring of 1870. Larger in scope, yet simpler and more focused, with only two main crossing points: Vermont-New York and Detroit.

And this time, total secrecy. No grandiose speechifying, no invasion funds, no rallies in Buffalo and pointing across the river at Canadian soil promising to "plant the flag of Irish freedom" there – as Roberts had done in the run-up to Ridgeway.

This time: shock and awe. (Major Henri le Caron dutifully took notes.)

Shoulder to shoulder

When last we saw the Atkinsons they were being surveilled in Port Huron by a Pinkerton detective. Now they emerge as members of John O'Neill's inner circle.

With the hero of Ridgeway now firmly in command, the Philadelphia convention in 1868 marked the high point of the Fenian movement – delegates from as far away as Nebraska and Montana attended. As reported in the *Philadelphia Age* on November 27, O'Neill and Fenian brass held "secret sessions at the Assembly Buildings during the week and important results have been anticipated by friends of Ireland all over the world."

At those sessions O'Neill laid out his plan for 1870. Unlike past congresses, where rival factions were bitterly divided, this time there was – in William Atkinson's typically understated language – "considerable enthusiasm."

The year before, William had succeeded his brother O'Brien as Head Centre of the Port Huron circle. Considering his illustrious war record and extensive knowledge of the western Ontario area (where he was born), William was placed second-in-command of the Detroit crossing, which was to be led by General John McDermott of Bay City. O'Neill would lead the main invasion from Vermont and northeastern New York state.

The climax of the convention was a Thanksgiving Day parade through downtown Philadelphia with marching bands and 3,000 Fenian soldiers, three full regiments, all sharply attired in new uniforms, under arms – with O'Neill and his top officers leading the way.

As reported by the *Philadelphia Age*, shoulder to shoulder with O'Neill at the front of the line was "aide de camp Lt. Col. John Atkinson."

And, of course, "Major Henry LeCaron" (sic).

It must have been a sight. In addition to those Fenian regiments, the newspaper reported a "handsome chariot drawn by six grey horses" and a high reviewing platform with an enormous brass bell "that kept tolling over the whole route of the procession." Another 5,000 Irish "civic leaders" marched. They wore "dark suits and badges and pieces of green ribbon tied in the button holes of their coats."

"The sidewalks were lined with expectant watchers... three and four abreast. The universal color was green... green badges, green neckties, green flags, green coats, green sashes, green uniforms... and the procession did not cease marching until the shades of evening approached."

"A banner was carried in the line of the civic societies, containing the following, in gold letters on a field of green satin:

Delegates – remember the words of our martyred O'Brien, to unite in God's name for Ireland and Liberty.

God save Ireland."

Acquired risk

Almost immediately, O'Neill's plan began to lose traction. The process of procuring and carefully secreting weapons moved slowly forward. Fenian leaders would later claim they had as many as 10,000 stand of arms in warehouses between Port Huron and Detroit, and five times that number in upstate New York. But meanwhile, the reality of everyday life for most Fenians – away from the boisterous meetings – began to assert itself.

A year and a half after Philadelphia, by the spring of 1870, there was a new President, a new Congress, a new Canadian confederation. "Reconstruction" was ending (or being abandoned), Southern states were being readmitted, expansion and settlement of the West was the new focus. True, there'd been no real abatement of anti-British feeling – the "Alabama

Claims" still dominated headlines – but people were moving on, building lives in their local communities, raising families.[1]

Before the first invasion, in 1866, most Fenians
were returning from long wartime service to a future uncertain.
But by 1870 they had jobs, children… in insurance
parlance they had "acquired risk."

As "the hour for action" in 1870 neared, unit commanders who had been chosen to great fanfare in Philadelphia began to realistically assess what they stood to lose. If things went wrong again, would the government be so forgiving this time? And nobody had forgotten those two dozen or so unfortunate Fenian prisoners, from the 1866 invasion, who were still doing hard-labor in Canada. The last one would not be released

---

1   It is not by chance that the erosion of rank-and-file Fenian fervor coincided with the creation of many municipal police forces and fire departments soon after the Civil War. A number of sociologists point to this. Previously unemployed Irish men all but monopolized these low-paying public-sector jobs when they were first developed. Irish after the war also found good work laying rails for street cars and railroads.

In time, a second generation of Irish laborers moved into the skilled trades. By the year 1900, when Irish American men comprised roughly a tenth of the male labor force, they represented almost a third of the plumbers, steamfitters and boilermakers.

until 1872.[1]

What's more, the near-obsessive (if futile) secrecy of Fenian leadership meant that no public momentum could be created. American readers (and editors) were growing tired of the story anyway. A review of local newspapers and national publications of the time shows continued coverage of Fenian activities – but the stories are sporadic, shorter and usually found on inside pages.

O'Brien Atkinson, now an established Port Huron city official, did not go.

Nor, apparently, did Colonel John Atkinson. Now a prominent young figure in Michigan law and politics, in 1870 the Colonel moved his practice to Detroit. He had marched with O'Neill in Philadelphia, but his role in the second invasion a year and half later is unclear.

Considering all of the above, why did William Atkinson go to war with Canada in 1870 – and end up with a £2,000

---

1   The last Fenian prisoner released by Canadian authorities was a priest who – like eight others – had originally been sentenced to death. Rev. John McMahon of Indiana was captured in a barn near Fort Erie ministering to wounded Fenian troops. At his trial in Toronto, the priest insisted that he'd been traveling east on personal business when he was kidnapped in Buffalo and forced to act as the Fenians' chaplain. Fenian circles in America held "indignation meetings" and sent protests to Toronto claiming Father McMahon had only been in engaged in "discharging his duties as a clergyman."

bounty on his head?

At age 24, his promising legal career was just starting. William quit school at 16 to enlist during the Civil War; now he was "reading law"[2] in the practices of older brothers John and O'Brien. He had also dabbled in the newspaper business, briefly publishing a weekly (with John) in Port Huron. But beyond these factors was a singular "acquired risk": his new wife. William married Katherine Donnelly – a Canadian – in February, 1870.

Scores of Fenian leaders and thousands of "soldiers" from Minnesota, Wisconsin and Illinois, from Michigan and Indiana, right across to New York and Vermont, at the last minute, bailed. William didn't. Why?

We need not speculate. William himself answered the question – in 1893 – in a lengthy interview with the *Detroit Tribune.* By then he was one of the Detroit's most well-known and admired lawyers: Atkinson Avenue downtown is named for him. An enterprising reporter dug up some old clips and asked him about this curious bit of history. He agreed to an interview.

---

2 "Reading law" was a widely-accepted form of legal apprenticeship in an era when accredited law schools were few and could not hope to supply the demand for lawyers.

"Those stormy days"

The *Detroit Tribune* article was dramatically headlined: "A Price Upon his Head... An Episode in the Life of William F. Atkinson."

As the interview begins, William sounds guarded. This is understandable. By 1893, more than a generation after its zenith, American Fenianism had evolved a negative cachet. Relations with Canada were becoming so cordial by the turn of the 20th century as to make the invasions of 1866 and 1870 slightly embarrassing. Having been a Fenian wasn't the sort of thing you wished to define your life.[1]

"It's been so long since those stormy days, I cannot recall

---

1   In their time, the Atkinson "quartet" acquired such news-value that each one's passing, in turn, was the subject of extensive commentary and homage. And in the case of Colonel John, the lavish news coverage went on for weeks. Yet obituary writers expended not a single line on the roles of O'Brien, John or William in the Fenian movement and 1870 invasion. This was probably not so much an omission as a courtesy.

John, in fact, met with Gladstone to discuss land reform in Ireland during his widely-publicized tour of the British Isles in 1889. This was prominently mentioned in John's obituaries – but not his Fenian past.

the proper dates," William protested. Instead he digresses into a long monologue about his Civil War record, as if to validate his American – rather than purely Irish – credentials.

But as the interview proceeds, he relaxes.

As we would expect, William gives his reason as the "call of the motherland to strike a blow at the old enemy of the Celt." (We can assume the *Tribune* writer dressed up this quote a bit, as was customary.) But deeper into the piece we find a man one researcher feels he has come to know: an old infantry soldier who instinctively deflects self-adornment. Instead he nostalgically recalls "the lads... the boys who marched side by side with me." Although clearly given the opportunity, he does not even mention William Smith O'Brien or speak of his family's connections to Irish nationalism.[2]

What emerges from William's interview is that "whole soul" quality Pinkerton's agent put his finger on: loyalty to comradeship and command. When we ask why William boarded that train for Buffalo – when so many "committed Fenians" stayed home in 1870 – the answer seems to be: because he said he would. And because he believed O'Neill would be waiting.

What also emerges from the interview is a glimpse of

---

2   In the interview, interestingly, William never mentioned his two "Fenian brothers" O'Brien or John.

William's deep personal connection to Canada.

The reader will recall Pinkerton's statement in 1868 that the Atkinson brothers "do not go into Canada." Clearly this was a blind spot in surveillance. As today, traffic between Port Huron and Sarnia was common. Like many professionals in Port Huron, the Atkinsons would often have had occasion to visit Sarnia for any number of reasons. We know that O'Brien sold Aetna insurance for a time, and may have been engaged briefly in import-export. John was the port customs inspector. William was involved in the newspaper business.

What's more, the Sarnia-Port Huron gateway was a busy point of immigration. New rail lines were being opened on both sides of the St. Clair River. Oil had been discovered near Sarnia in the late 1850s.

Exactly how and when William first made the acquaintance of Kate Donnelly, we do not know. Her family lived not far from Sarnia, in the township of Plympton, on a large and prosperous farm identified on the original plats as "Donnelly's Corners" (because the property fronted all four corners of intersecting Lambton County roads). Kate was one of 12 children, a daughter of William and Eleanor (Bolger) Donnelly, whose immigrant story is similar to that of the Atkinsons.

During the interview William reached into his pocket – this is nearly 25 years later – and produced "a time-worn document." It was his Commission in the army of the "Irish Republic." He showed it to the reporter but quickly cautioned, "I don't want to lose that old paper... even my Canadian wife is anxious to preserve a record of my rank in the army that invaded her country."

Kate and William were married at the Donnelly home, February 28, 1870. Less than three months later he was rushing to New York to rendezvous with O'Neill, and what he must have felt was destiny.

What "saved Canada for England"

What if – in 1866 or 1870 – the Fenians had had a few thousand more like O'Neill and Atkinson? Men who simply showed up and followed through. Historians relish a good counter-factual. So do military veterans. In his 1893 interview we find William offering a succinct analysis:

> "The American government gave us lots of time to accomplish
> our end," he told the *Tribune* reporter. "But the inaction
> of some of the (Fenian) leaders and delays and postponements
> (are what) saved Canada for England."

Some would say this is the nutshell summary of the entire Fenian story: They had their chance. There is no hint of intended irony in William's comment. He seems to believe those last four words. And as far as 1866 is concerned, when the Fenians were given "five full days," he may even be right.

But for 1870?

The newly confederated Canadian provinces passed a Militia Act in October, 1868 – around the same time O'Neill was marching at the head of that glorious 3,000-man Fenian brigade in Philadelphia. As a result, Canada had 40,000 well-trained and well-equipped "active militia" ready to deploy on a moment's notice. And where "those damned Fenians" were concerned, this new Canadian force was imbued with a bring-it-on mindset.[1]

Canadian militia units were led and advised by a small cadre of professional British officers, all keen for battle, and bolstered by garrisons of the Queen's Own.

Nevertheless on paper – again – the Fenian strategy was feasible.

The plan called for at least 1,000 Fenians led by the "Michigan Division" to converge on Detroit (arriving in small groups, incognito). On the designated day they would cross to Windsor in force, engage any opposing militia, seize rail transportation and cut all lines of communication... but ensuring that local officials had time to telegraph distress calls to Ottawa. This diversionary raid would be sufficiently large to force a response from the provincial capital. (Port Huron was ruled out as a crossing point. So large a number of arriving troops would be too obvious to river sentries in Sarnia.)

---

1   Historian W. S. Niedhardt, whose *Fenianism in North America* is written from a Canadian point of view, cites several Canadian politicians who, in speeches before their parliament, taunted and openly invited the Fenians to attempt another invasion.

Meanwhile, an overwhelming main Fenian invasion force would cross on land – *on land*, not by river again with all the complications of barges and scows – from Vermont and north-eastern New York directly into Quebec province.

In 1866 Sweeny bragged he could "do the job" with only 10,000 men. O'Neill wanted twice that number: at least 20,000 Fenians were committed to the fight from circles along the East Coast and New England. O'Neill's forces would swiftly capture St. Jean, south of Montreal, and Richmond, nestled against the Green Mountains. This would give him total command of a significant piece of geography between the St. Lawrence Seaway and the American border.

Equally important, O'Neill would have a virtually unassailable position from which to defend against counter-attack. Canadians would themselves have to mount a complex, hazardous river crossing (across the St. Lawrence) to dislodge the Fenians.

Never mind a march on Montreal or Ottawa: not necessary. Once O'Neill had achieved these few modest objectives, the St. Lawrence would become untenable for commerce. The entire southern bank of the river in Quebec would now be Fenian territory, from which O'Neill's artillery officers could harass British shipping at their leisure. Canada would in theory grind to an economic standstill.

If the U. S. government simply recognized "accomplished

facts," the British would have no choice but to start negotiating.

No one seriously imagined that Ulysses S. Grant or any president could send federal troops – in earnest – against a large Fenian occupying force in Canada. To send Americans against Americans, only five years after the Civil War, was not an option. If the Fenians could hold their piece of Quebec, it would be months before England could mount any kind of trans-Atlantic military undertaking. And by then how many Americans would have rallied to the Fenian cause?

This was the prospect – the outside chance a Fenian force might succeed in seizing a chunk of Canada – that preoccupied the governments of Canada, England and America.

But as always in war, everything depended on timing. When, where and how many men would show up?

William picks up the story from here:

"When the day for action began to draw near, Colonel McDermott[1] backed out for some unaccountable reason," William said. "This wavered several of the rank and file. But

---

1 John McDermott returned from the Civil War a full colonel. He made his home in Bay City and "reaped the fullest measure of success and the confidence and respect of all good citizens," according to a history of Bay County in the Michigan Historical Society. Presumably he chose not to risk his standing.

there were those of us resolved to join O'Neill with whatever force we could muster. And so I was appointed in command of the Michigan division and left Port Huron one Saturday night (May 21) with a large army – just fifteen men."

"Arriving in Detroit my force was augmented to about 75, but that did not encourage us much as we were expecting at least 500 from the city. Old Justice of the Peace John Patton[1] was among the gang who joined us there. Also a J.P. McDonegal... who is now in Kansas City."

"There was another young fellow... Phelan... who if I am not mistaken is a member of the Montgomery Guards[2] of this city. There were others whose names I do not know but they salute me now whenever I meet them on the streets... and I recognize them as having belonged to my command."

"We went from here to Toledo by way of the Lake Shore

---

1   In 1788, when Michigan was still the Northwest Territory, a system of Justices of the Peace was created. By 1870 this had evolved to a circuit of small-claims judges, handling issues of less than $100 in damages.

Like William Atkinson and most other Fenian leaders, Patton suffered no tangible repercussions for his role in 1870. He was elected Senior Justice of the Peace for Detroit in 1880.

2   The Montgomery Guards was one of numerous "militia" organizations formed prior to the Civil War and which, afterward, continued as private clubs.

and Michigan Southern. At Toledo we got another reinforcement of several hundred... and that encouraged us... that Canada really could be taken."[3]

"In Buffalo we were reinforced by about 500 and were tendered a reception... the people turning out en masse to welcome us. Next day we moved to Rome, New York, where we got the largest reinforcement of all."

Rome was one of four staging areas for the New York-Vermont crossing.

---

3   These were some of the men originally scheduled to arrive in Detroit but now stranded in Toledo without a senior officer. They quickly joined Atkinson's command. At this point Atkinson and his patchwork regiment believed they would link up in New York with perhaps 20,000 men.

Common cause

We arrive now at the one of the more cinematic aspects of the American Fenian movement – that of Confederate soldiers joining forces with Union veterans, Irish all.[1]

When he arrived in Rome on May 24th, Atkinson

---

1 Perhaps 40,000 Irish fought for the Confederacy – less than a third the total number in Northern armies. This is not surprising, as the North enjoyed a population advantage in every respect. We say "perhaps." Exact numbers have defied generations of researchers. The victorious Northern states invested a great deal of time annotating "regimental histories." But in the ruined South there were other priorities. Many war records remain incomplete.

Many of these veterans were Catholic, but in the South a comparatively larger percentage of Irish were Protestant with deep American roots. In the early 1700s thousands of Ulster Presbyterian dissenters (originally of Scottish descent) were driven out of Ireland and eventually settled in the Appalachian regions of what were then British colonies. Many of these British-hating Scots-Irish found "common cause" with the Fenians who – after the war – established circles in virtually all major Southern cities.

A side note: the famous Irish Brigades of Northern armies were composed largely of poor or lower middle class Catholics. Often entire Fenian circles enlisted. The South too had its Irish Brigades – but these were generally smaller squadrons of "elite" cavalry, and Protestant to a man.

encountered "a Fenian company from Louisville, Kentucky – and they were the finest company I ever saw. All of them were former Confederate soldiers and when they reported to me as the commanding officer I informed their captain that I was a Union soldier in the war."

"At this he shook my hand three times as warmly and remarked: 'Well, Colonel, we are fighting now for a common cause.' The men overheard the captain's remark and the lads who were the Blue shook the hands of the lads who were the Gray and made the city ring with their merry-making all night long."

"I don't think I will ever forget the impression of that meeting of the Blue and the Gray," William said.

"Most of the men who made up the (Fenian) Michigan and Ohio contingents had been in the thick of the fight to save the Union... many of them had experienced the horrors of Southern prisons (including Atkinson himself, at Danville). Yet as members of our race who rallied to the call of the motherland... they forgot for the time being there had ever been a war between North and South," William said.

But while Atkinson and his now sizable regiment of Blue and Gray veterans were "singing songs through the streets" in Rome, O'Neill was in despair.

On the morning of May 24th, at his covert headquarters in St. Albans, Vermont, O'Neill met the train from Boston.

He was expecting more than 1,000 men. Fewer than 50 stepped off. Then the eastern New York contingent reported: one-sixth the promised number, not even 100 men. All day the news dribbled in by telegraph. Delays here, no-shows there, defections of officers.

O'Neill was not aware that Atkinson's combined force had already arrived in Rome. He called a desperate meeting of his officers and decided to drop the Richmond-St. Jean plan – not nearly enough men – and instead try for a smaller crossing from Franklin, New York. He had perhaps 500 men.

At this point O'Neill was hoping only to secure a slender lodgement and hold on for reinforcements, which he was assured were still coming. Time was slipping away.

With the commotion around St. Albans, O'Neill worried that he'd lost the element of surprise. He'd lost it days earlier. Alerted by Le Caron and other spies, Canadian militia were carefully preparing defenses at all likely crossing points. O'Neill also was being pursued by a United States Marshal, George Foster, with orders for his arrest.

Meanwhile, the Atkinson Regiment was following the original plan.

"We left Rome at daybreak for Malone, New York, the next day. (Malone was a launch point for the crossing into Quebec.) Several thousand stand of arms were stored there," William said. "The boys were mad for a fight and they were craving to get those arms into their hands. I had fully fifteen-hundred men under my command and the anticipation of a scrap with the old enemy of our race put them in an excellent fighting humor."

Once decamped in Malone, Atkinson "dispatched messengers to O'Neill to inform him that we were ready and giving him all the particulars as to our strengths and equipments (sic). We waited anxiously all day for a reply. The men began to get impatient and clamored to advance on the Canadian front at once."

No word arrived on May 25th. Atkinson waited. He held to O'Neill's original orders for the Malone contingent: to wait until O'Neill had safely crossed. Finally at dawn the next day, a courier rode in with news that O'Neill was "preparing to cross." Atkinson said "the men began to feel good again at this intelligence."

But in fact, O'Neill had "bungled."

At his new camp near Franklin, a flabbergasted O'Neill was confronted that morning by U. S. Marshal Foster, accompanied only by a terrified deputy. Foster burst into O'Neill's tent, curtly identified himself and read out a proclamation signed by President Grant warning "all good citizens against aiding, countenancing, abetting or taking part in unlawful proceedings" in violation of the Neutrality Act. O'Neill's astonished aides formed a human wall around the general, preventing his immediate arrest.

At this Foster departed – for the Canadian border less than a mile away. There he met with commanders of the entrenched militia units and warned them a crossing was imminent.

A few hours later, incredibly, O'Neill crossed. A wooden bridge spanned the border. The instant O'Neill's men passed the median point on it, Canadians opened fire from scores of concealed positions on Eccles Hill. One Fenian was killed and several more wounded. The vanguard hesitated... then retreated headlong to O'Neill's camp, leaving the general at the bridge trying to rally his men. Just that quickly, it was over.

To punctuate the fiasco, Foster and his deputy caught up again with O'Neill as he was tending to a wounded man in a nearby barn. Foster arrested him on the spot and whisked O'Neill away in a closed carriage – right past two columns of dazed Fenians.

Atkinson and his 1,500 men in nearby Malone were still waiting for word.

"Around noon a messenger apprised me of the fact that O'Neill had been arrested by U. S. authorities," Atkinson told the *Tribune*. "The men cursed O'Neill for making a bungle, as they called it."

"Several of the (senior) men suggested we advance on the Canadian frontier with our own force... but it was too late.

The United States government had taken a decisive step to prevent the move on Canada. We received orders from headquarters (New York City) to disband and we did so... not without feeling bitter disappointment and anger."[1]

"I often think that no army ever retreated from battle with a greater feeling of humiliation," Atkinson said.

ATKINSON'S COMMENTS ARE TELLING. His immediate decision to stand down – and O'Neill's quiescent surrender – reflect the fact that under no circumstances would most Fenians have crossed the U. S. government (nor even a solitary representative of federal authority such as the redoubtable George Foster). On the contrary, the Fenians consistently believed the government was their silent ally, and that the majority of Americans were their supporters.

This complete misread of the American political environment was adroitly summed up in 1947 by Fenian scholar William D'Arcy:

---

1 A renegade force of roughly 450 Fenians, not connected with the Atkinson Brigade, did cross the Canadian border on May 26, capturing a telegraph office and establishing camp near Huntingdon.

But leaderless and confused, they were quickly repulsed by the approach of several thousand combined militia and British regulars.

"The Fenians made the natural (immigrant) mistake of construing anti-English feeling as a (sincerely) pro-Irish sentiment..."

"Anti-Irish sentiment was certainly as strong as anti-English, but with a difference. The one was directed against Irishmen, not against Ireland. And the other was directed against England, but not against Englishmen."

"Estranged from the main body of Americans by their religion, Irish immigrants were welcome in America because the country needed their labor, and were especially welcome to the politicians who found their votes useful on election day," D'Arcy wrote.

The Atkinson brothers did grasp these distinctions, of course, and they would prove skillful in negotiating the American legal, political and social landscape for the rest of their lives. But not before an object lesson in 1870.

"2,000 plump sovereigns"

Within days, the Canadian government drew up a slate of "Fenian leaders" to be arrested and extradited for trial in Toronto – with extravagant bounties assigned for those at the top of the list. This was public relations. O'Neill, for whom the Canadians promised 5,000 pounds sterling, was already in American custody. Ditto his officers from the Franklin debacle.

Fenian Lieutenant Colonel William Atkinson, who by now was on his way home to Port Huron, was identified as "second in command" and tagged with a £2,000 bounty. It made for a good *Tribune* headline 25 years later, but was never a real concern.

O'Neill, on the other hand, had problems. He was still incarcerated in Burlington, Vermont. A commissioner set his bond at a staggering $20,000. At this point Fenian leaders around the country (most of whom had stayed home), embarrassed by O'Neill's failure and stung by a suddenly scornful media, abandoned the general. No official effort was made to raise funds for his release.

Months later, in his verbose 1870 "Report of the Attempted Invasion of Canada," an embittered O'Neill spoke of languishing day after day in his jail cell "very much hurt by this neglect."[1]

Here we see Atkinson's rescue reflex. When O'Neill's difficulty became known, William in Port Huron and a handful of other top Fenians in Wisconsin, Minnesota and New York, pooled their personal funds and wired the money to Vermont. O'Neill was so moved by this gesture that in his report he listed each bail contributor by name – to gouge those who'd refused to help. It was a short list, only half a dozen contributors.

---

1 O'Neill was convicted of violating Neutrality Laws and sentenced to two years in prison. He served only a few months. Yet again, the government intervened. In October of 1870 the British – still anxious about the "Alabama Claims" and desiring rapprochement with the U. S. – proposed that all Fenian prisoners in Canada and America be freed. President Grant pardoned all eight Fenian leaders in American prisons. But the Canadians balked. They held the last of their 1866-invasion prisoners until 1872.

Authorities eventually found and seized 25 wagonloads of arms and munitions around Malone and Franklin. If not "for want of men" the 1870 invasion had every chance to succeed, O'Neill affirmed. He blamed "thousands of men indulging their doubts... until it was too late to be of service."

What's interesting is that O'Neill[2] thanked "Colonel Wm. F. Atkinson and Brother, Port Huron, Michigan" for posting his bond. But which brother? Most likely, John. William had not yet established a law practice, but by this time John was successful and financially capable. He was also becoming quite a real estate speculator.

Which brings us to a little town in Nebraska...

---

2   John O'Neill never stopped tilting at Canada. In October, 1871, one year after his release from prison in Vermont, the general led another raid into Canada. This time in Manitoba. It was by far the most bizarre episode of O'Neill's invasion trilogy. To begin with, the raid was not a Fenian-sanctioned venture and had nothing to do with Irish liberty. O'Neill in fact was hitchhiking on a Manitoba independence movement composed of native Metis people and pioneer settlers, led by the Canadian folk hero Louis Riel and one of Riel's associates, William O'Donoghue.

O'Donoghue had come to the now-arthritic Fenian Brotherhood asking for manpower and support. The New York circle – weary of the name Canada – rejected his plan. The vote was nearly unanimous. The only dissenter: John O'Neill.

A few weeks later, with four dozen mercenaries and self-styled Canadian rebels, O'Neill was captured at a Manitoba border trading post by a troop of American cavalry dispatched from Fort Pembina.

PART 5

"A big black stallion no one else could handle"

Our travelogue had taken us from County Mayo to Halifax, from Michigan to Tennessee, back again to Canada via New York, with stops in Texas and Philadelphia, Atlanta and Buffalo, to name only a few. It seems fitting that we should post a vignette from – why not? – Nebraska.

Today, in the broad farm country of north central Nebraska, near the Elkhorn River, situated alongside U. S. Highway 20, stand the communities of Atkinson and O'Neill. There are two versions of how they got there.

The authorized romantic story is that while sitting despondently in his Vermont jail cell, O'Neill conceived a new Irish "liberation" plan. He would establish Irish colonies in the virgin American West, transplanting whole communities from the squalid mining towns and hopeless slums of the East to unlimited opportunities on the frontier. Here the Catholic Irish could build their own churches and schools, operate their own local governments, and live free from discrimination. They could start again from scratch.

The other version is that after his Manitoba raid in 1871 O'Neill traveled around the west and realized he could make a personal fortune through land speculation.

Homestead "sections" were generally free to those who would stay and build and work the land. But railroads were money. As the various lines wound westward, rail magnates either leased or bought vast tracks of property along the way. What's more, coaling stations were needed. The key was to anticipate railroad construction and get there first. Of course this venture capital model was widely known. The difference for O'Neill was that he could create complete functioning towns in advance of the rail lines – presto – by bringing colonies of Irish west.[1]

Whatever his motives the plan eventually succeeded – almost despite O'Neill, and with a nudge from Colonel John Atkinson.

O'Neill still had enormous star power amongst the

---

1   Some writers have suggested O'Neill hoped these frontier Irish colonies would become "base camps" from which he could recruit and train a new revolutionary army. Manitoba and the northwest territories of Canada were still resisting union with the Canadian Confederation. A separate Irish colony in South Dakota, possibly a prototype for O'Neill's concept, had been settled in 1869. Anglophobe town leaders openly spoke of waiting for the "right time" to strike again into British North America.

"miserable, friendless" Irish of Eastern cities and he embarked on a lecture circuit touting the "splendid land, pure water and healthy climate" awaiting Irish on the frontier. "No part of the West offers so many advantages to settlers and particularly to Irish Americans... as Holt County, Nebraska." The venerable *Irish World* even donated full-page space to advertise O'Neill's colonization scheme. He made the sale.[2]

The first of O'Neill's intrepid colonists – 13 men, two women, five children – arrived at Holt County in May, 1874. They'd journeyed for weeks by rail as far as Wisner, the end of the line, then by wagon the remaining 60 miles. Now they stood more or less slack-jawed at the vista of endless flat empty space "fifty miles from a post office... a hundred miles from civilization... without a doctor or teacher or priest."

O'Neill reportedly tried to lift spirits by reminding the Irish that the soil was fertile, the game plentiful and "the Indians were friendly." Dissension set in immediately. But just as quickly this was tempered by reality: the settlers were

---

2 O'Neill handed out pamphlets outlining precisely what each pioneer family would need. Among the items: "temporary house, $50 to 75; team of oxen, 80 to 125; breaking plow, 24 to 30; corn planter, 2 to 3; other tools, 10 to 15; stove, 24 to 30; cooking utensils, 10 to 20; cheap (sic) furniture, 20 to 30; cash for expenses, 50 to 100." The estimated total for a new life in Nebraska was between $270 and $428.

now a thousand miles from home and virtually broke (having purchased their supplies in Omaha and Wisner). They were, as poker players say, all in.

Within a week, colonists put up the first edifice in what is now O'Neill, Nebraska, a sod and sagebrush structure they called the "Grand Central Hotel." Such humor saw them through until only a few months later — in what must have seemed an act of Providence — Custer's expedition confirmed the discovery of gold in the Black Hills. O'Neill's colony was instantly transformed into a way station and supply depot: at one point during the rush of the late 1870s, a general store in O'Neill was doing $1,000 a day in business.

The gold rush also sent General O'Neill into ecstasies of land speculation. He bought tracks of land for future colonies up and down various proposed rail lines, almost none of which were developed. By 1876, he was in debt and sending telegrams to Detroit.

Enter the Colonel.

WE CAN SURMISE THAT William Atkinson had had enough of O'Neill's ventures.

But by the late 1870s his brother Colonel John, well established in Detroit, was beginning a side career as a property investor. Eventually he would build a vacation home on Mackinac (which still stands) and own practically all of Bois Blanc island, which later became famous as Bob-Lo amusement park, the playground of Detroit. In Nebraska he saw a chance to advance the Irish Catholic cause – and acquire his own town in the bargain.

It is unclear whether the Colonel bought out "his friend" O'Neill's deeds or made the distressed acquisition separately, but in 1877 Atkinson arrived in the Elkhorn Valley and created a stir among Irish colonists.

In memoirs Atkinson is described as "a stalwart military man. He wore his black hair long and rode a big black stallion no one else could handle."

Upon that black stallion Atkinson proceeded to plat his new town. "He had the land surveyed into city blocks and sub-divided into lots, all marked by cedar stakes," according to a Holt County history. "A furrow was broken around the entire quarter section, then two furrows (denoting) a street running east and west. These furrows were plowed the full length of the piece. This was to be the main street..."

What attracted Atkinson to this section of land, less than 20 miles west of O'Neill, was a preliminary survey by the Fremont, Elkhorn & Missouri Valley Railroad. Their proposed tracks went straight through the Colonel's new property. But once again, an Atkinson was snake-bitten by O'Neill.

The railroad eventually decided that the southern half of the Colonel's section was too low and swampy. Each spring, "rains made the land totally unsuitable." It turned out to be 60 acres of "buffalo wallows."

"Not a building of any kind ever graced a single lot" of Atkinson's carefully platted "town." Yet directly across the Elkhorn River on higher ground, a kind of ad hoc community of Irish laborers had slowly developed. No plat. No organization. Even today, the town of Atkinson is remarkable for widely separated buildings and angular property lines. This accidental town thrived.

A leader of the unnamed community, Frank Bitney, offered the railroad 40 acres of his own land if they would run their tracks on the other side of the river. The railroad accepted. But in preparing the paperwork, there was one issue: what to call this place? Bitney, who had befriended the Colonel, decided to name the town Atkinson in his honor.

Although he took pride in the town that adopted his name, Nebraska became hardly more than a footnote in the

Colonel's life – far eclipsed by 20 subsequent years of state politics, courtroom conquests and scandalous episodes. He never returned.

But for John O'Neill, his Irish colonies brought a measure of the immortality he'd craved. He was traveling through Arkansas, scouting more possible locations, when he caught a cold and then suffered a stroke. At a hospital in Omaha, he died of complications from pneumonia in 1878. He was 44.

Today there is monument at O'Neill's gravesite in Omaha, not erected until 1919.

Last of Famed Quartet of Lawyer Brothers

By GEORGE W. STARK

The last of the Atkinson boys died in his sleep Wednesday and now all that remains of a gallant quartet of soldiering and lawing brothers are the precious mementoes of the town, permanent testimonials that they were once vital factors in our physical and sentimental fabric. Such monuments as the Atkinson School, Atkinson avenue and the Atkinson Playground are bound to prove more enduring than works of stone or metal.

James J. Atkinson was the last brother to go. The three who preceded him were O'Brien J. Atkinson, Col. John Atkinson and William F. Atkinson.

James J. was 92 years old when death came quietly to him after a long life of more than normal activity. He was at his home, 4336 Avery avenue.

These brothers were bound more closely together than even the ties

—By News Staff Photographer

JAMES J. ATKINSON, last of four famous brothers, all soldiers and lawyers, died Wednesday at the age of 92.

(Above) Last of the "gallant quartet," James J. Atkinson obituary, Detroit News, 1940.

Plate 1

(Above) O'Brien J. Atkinson, 1839 – 1901: first graduate of the University of Michigan Law School, 1860; twice-elected County prosecutor, St. Clair County, Michigan (Port Huron); first president of Village of Fort Gratiot; Vice President of the American Bar Association; President of the Michigan Bar Association; organizer and first "Head Centre" of the Fenian Brotherhood "circle" in Port Huron; noted lawyer and legal scholar, Circuit Court judge, civic leader (chairman of the Port Huron Library Board) and philanthropist. In 1864, O'Brien attempted to join his brothers in uniform but Michigan had by then met its quota of 90,000 volunteers.

(Above right) Irish revolutionist William Smith O'Brien, 1803 – 1864: a distant relative (on the maternal side) of the Atkinsons and namesake of O'Brien Atkinson. What made O'Brien unique and so beloved among Young Ireland activists was that he was a Protestant landowner who stood to gain nothing from Catholic land reform. Beyond their claim to blood ties, it seems the Atkinson family of Port Huron felt a special bond with O'Brien (his name has endured through five generations of O'Brien Atkinson). This may have its basis in the Catholic Atkinsons' own obscure Protestant Irish origins.

Plate 2

Launch Point for Invasion: Port Huron, Michigan, circa 1867:

Port Huron in the late 1860s was home to one of the nation's most aggressive Fenian "circles" led by the Atkinson brothers: O'Brien, John and William. Federal government spies and Canadian officials believed a second Fenian invasion of British North America could start here – with a crossing directly into Sarnia or a river landing at points south. This rendering (by Alfred Ruger) presents an energetic young Port Huron in the foreground with Sarnia on the Canadian side, divided by the busy St. Clair River and Lake Huron beyond. Port Huron itself is bisected by the Black River. Illustrated are many lumber mills and a new train depot at the docks. The "thumb" of Michigan may seem an unlikely place to launch the liberation of Ireland. But for the Fenians it was considered a critical western flank.

Plate 3

(Above left) John Atkinson, 1841 – 1898: Graduated University of Michigan Law School two years after brother O'Brien, 1862; Captain and commander Company C, 22nd Michigan; ended the war as Lt. Colonel, 3rd Michigan; in 1870 relocated from Port Huron to Detroit; close friend of O'Neill and the Fenian cause, but later an influential moderate voice for Irish nationalism.

Widely (if sometimes grudgingly) admired by legal peers and known for his "aggressive disposition," the Colonel was as an expert on criminal and libel law. He twice successfully defended the Detroit News – then later brought suit *against* the same paper and won. Near the turn of the century he was a key advisor to Detroit Mayor (later Governor) Hazen Pingree *(above right)*. In 1897 he won a seat in the state Assembly for the express purpose of advancing Pingree's agenda. The landmark Atkinson Bill, which reformed corporate and railroad tax rates, was passed posthumously. Pingree considered it his greatest achievement.

Even in death, the Colonel was controversial. Capitalizing on his fame and scandalous affair with socialite Josephine Caspari, in whose home he died, in 1898 a cigar company issued the Colonel Atkinson Cigar with labels bearing his well-known likeness. Atkinson's humiliated widow Lida filed suit. But the state Supreme Court held that an individual's image "is not personal property" subject to "actionable wrong." This set in motion decades of "publicity rights" cases, eventually leading to legal protections that public figures take for granted today.

Plate 4

(Above) Sergeant William F. Atkinson (back row, far right) and Captain John Atkinson (next to William, looking to his right) with members of Company C, 22nd Michigan Infantry, atop Lookout Mountain in 1863, prior to the Battle of Chickamauga. Seated casually at the cliff face is believed to be the company mascot and "Drummer Boy of Chickamauga," Johnny Clem.

(Left) Said to be the youngest "soldier" in U. S. military history, 13-year old drummer boy Johnny Clem was rejected as under-age by several other units before he was adopted by Company C and later mustered in by Captain Atkinson (who passed a hat to collect Clem's "pay"). A few weeks later at Chickamauga, Clem discarded his drum kit for a rifle and fired on a Confederate officer attempting to take him prisoner – a story that made him an instant national hero. Clem survived the war, made a career of the army and eventually retired as a general.

Plate 5

(Top left) William F. Atkinson, 1846 – 1907: Sergeant, Company C, 22nd
Michigan Infantry and Acting 2nd Lt. at Chickamauga, where he was
wounded and captured; escaped Confederate prison at Danville *(above)*
and trekked 300 miles back to Union lines; signal officer for General
William Tecumseh Sherman *(top right)* during Sherman's march through
Georgia, mustered out as Captain, 3rd Michigan; succeeded brother
O'Brien as head centre of Port Huron Fenian circle, commanded 1,500-man
brigade of former Union and Confederate soldiers in the 1870 invasion
of Canada; sought for extradition by Canadian officials offering a £2,000
bounty. In later life a successful and "socially popular" Detroit attorney.

Plate 6

Gray and Blue in Common Cause: Although the Fenian movement was dominated by Irish Catholic veterans of the Union armies, a significant number of former Confederate units *(above)* joined the Brotherhood in common cause for Irish liberty. In May of 1870, one company of Kentucky Fenians joined the Atkinson Brigade at Rome, New York – the "finest company I ever saw," William Atkinson later said.

An interesting distinction: most northern Fenian officers were ex-infantry of middle class urban backgrounds (like the Atkinsons), but the majority of southern Fenian officers had enjoyed higher social status – among them former plantation owners – and had served in prestigious cavalry units.

Plate 7

(Above left) James J. Atkinson, 1848 – 1940, at age 90: enlisted at age 17 in the reconstituted 3rd Michigan (commanded by his brother John); served under Sheridan in Tennessee and Custer *(above right)* in Texas (as adjutant); mustered out in 1865 as a 1st Lieutenant.

(Above) Union forces (James among them) encamped at Nashville, December, 1864. The Battle of Nashville destroyed the Army of Tennessee as an effective Confederate fighting force and marked the end of large-scale engagements in the Western theater.

Plate 8

(Above left) James was among the first graduating class of Port Huron High School. He then studied in Europe, receiving a Ph.D. from the University of Innsbruck and attended law school at the University of Leipzig.

(Above right) Known around town as "Al", Thomas Edison was a boyhood pal of James Atkinson, who delivered newspapers the young entrepreneur printed aboard the daily train between Port Huron and Detroit.

(Above) The legal scholar of the family, James specialized in real estate law. As head of Michigan Investment Company, he owned or managed properties throughout Detroit and near the old Irish enclave of Corktown, where an acquaintance, Henry Ford, developed his prototype automobile.

Plate 9

At the Battle of Chickamauga, September, 1863, Confederate forces under Braxton Bragg *(left)* and James Longstreet *(right)* stopped a broad-based Union offensive along the border of southern Tennessee and northwestern Georgia. Although Chickamauga tactically was a Union defeat, the Atkinsons' 22nd Michigan and two other regiments – by holding the right flank into the night as other Union forces withdrew – helped prevent a catastrophic rout. The future Fenian commander William F. Atkinson was wounded and captured at Horseshoe Ridge along with brother Patrick, who died in Andersonville.

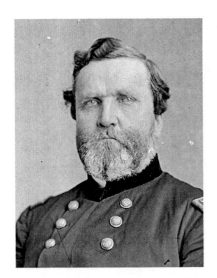

The "Rock of Chickamauga," General George H. Thomas *(left)*. While other units of Rosecrans' army retreated, Thomas ordered his Reserve Corps (including the 22nd Michigan, which was virtually wiped out) to close gaps in the line and hold their positions. Future president James Garfield, then a field officer, told a chastened Rosecrans that Thomas was "standing like a rock." After Gettysburg, Chickamauga was the single bloodiest engagement of the Civil War.

Plate 10

(Above) Commanding officers of the famed "Fighting 69th", one of several Irish Brigades. (The University of Notre Dame likely inherited the regiment's other nickname, "The Fighting Irish", after 69th chaplain Fr. William Corby served as the university's third president.) Irish nationalist leaders hoped America's Civil War would harden tens of thousands of Irish-American soldiers for the coming crusade against England.

(Above left) Brevet Brigadier General James Mulligan of Chicago, commander of the 23rd Illinois Irish Brigade and likely future Fenian leader (had he survived the Civil War). *(Above right)* Mulligan's classmate, close friend and staunch anti-Fenian Rt. Rev. John McMullen. It was Father McMullen who gave Mulligan's eulogy in 1864. Ironically, McMullen's niece would later marry Fenian leader William Atkinson's son.

Plate 11

Detroit in 1870 – the year the "Atkinson boys" hit town:

William Atkinson arrived here by rail on May 21, 1870, leading a contingent of Fenian raiders to join O'Neill's misbegotten second invasion of Canada. A few months later, Colonel John Atkinson opened his practice in Detroit – which quickly became a crucible for sensational cases and star legal careers (several of the Colonel's young associates went on to prominence, including the state Supreme Court). Younger brother (now ex-Fenian) William joined John in Detroit and briefly shared law offices before establishing his own practice. Three years later, the European-educated James also relocated to Detroit. (O'Brien, although active in state politics, never left Port Huron.)

The Atkinsons were a force in Detroit's economic, political and cultural life. Atkinson Avenue – now an historic district and once a marquee address for Detroit notables such as Ty Cobb – is named for William. Atkinson Park was donated to the city by James, and Atkinson Elementary School was named for James' partner and nephew Edmund.

But for 20 years the Colonel's exploits stole most of the headlines. In an era when legal oratory was considered high art, his summations regularly packed courtrooms with acolytes and rivals. He helped developed Detroit's Grand Boulevard: at first ridiculed as "Atkinson's Folly" but later the envy of urban planners who compared it to boulevards of Paris. And with partner James Randall he acquired, then bitterly feuded over Bois Blanc Island, which became the beloved day-trip amusement park known as Bob-Lo.

Plate 12

PART 6

The two Irelands:
Lunch with Gladstone and the legacy of Fenianism

The dateline now is London... Whitehall Gardens... fall of 1889.

One exceptionally sunny afternoon the American lawyer and Irish nationalist Colonel John Atkinson of Detroit – who 20 years earlier had marched with O'Neill in Philadelphia as plans were laid for a second Fenian invasion of British North America – was warmly received at the old mansion of former British Prime Minister Sir Robert Peel. Atkinson, the sole American, and a dozen other carefully chosen luncheon guests from the House of Lords and London society were ushered into the spacious dining room and seated at a large circular table. The chair at the Colonel's left remained empty.

Several minutes later, in strode the former and future Prime Minister William Gladstone. The great Liberal warhorse was now 79, but the Colonel recalled him as "youthful in all his ways." Gladstone shook hands all around then seated himself beside Atkinson. Over the next two hours, neither man touched his food. Gladstone was anxious to hear Atkinson's opinions of the American political scene and the sentiment among moderate American Irish leaders for "Home Rule" in Ireland – a sea-change in British policy that Gladstone had fought for (and lost) once, and would do so again.

This cordial tableau would have been unthinkable a generation before. Here was a prominent ex-Fenian invited to dine in the belly of the beast.

For many conservatives in British government and society, Atkinson and "his kind" were still considered, at best, bag men for a criminal Irish syndicate, if not accomplices in murder. In fact the Colonel and his traveling companion, Father Charles O. Reilly, treasurer of the Irish Land League and a Fenian-successor group known as Clan-na-Gael, had been under close (albeit inept) surveillance by Scotland Yard from the moment they arrived in London.[1]

Six years earlier, two of England's appointed overlords in Ireland, the Chief Secretary and Permanent Undersecretary

---

1   An amusing sidebar: Colonel Atkinson had little patience for intrigue. After several days of being tailed around London, he and Father Reilly appeared in the offices of Scotland Yard demanding to know the meaning of "this espionage." Stunned detectives told him the surveillance was due to "publications in America concerning the purpose of their visit. (But) after that he was no longer molested," according to a report in the Chicago Tribune, which noted that the Colonel had "bearded the lion in his den."

for Ireland, were hacked to death in a London park by Irish militants with suspected links to Clan-na-Gael. These so-called "Phoenix Park murders" were part of a dynamiting and assassination campaign that had reached to the House of Commons itself, where "Cabinet Ministers hardly trusted themselves to walk down St. James Street, after dark, unguarded." The Tower of London and London Bridge also were bombed.

By contrast, the invasions of Canada now seemed almost genteel. During the American Fenian era of the Atkinson brothers' younger days, even the most hated politicians were off limits, as were innocent civilians. No more. Nationalism had spawned a virulent, thuggish subculture. While a new generation of elected Irish leaders such as Charles Parnell championed the slow-but-steady political course toward Irish independence – forging alliances with Gladstone and like-minded liberals – a small shadow group ratcheted up the violence, seeming to relish the killing more than the cause.

This new Jekyll and Hyde split-personality in the Irish front had two effects: first, it undermined the political process by giving Protestant landlords and conservative M.P.s a plausible argument that native Catholic Irish – "not unlike the American Indians" – could never be trusted to govern or economically fend for themselves (a classic British colonial canard). To be sure, the conservatives would never have supported Irish Home Rule under any circumstances, but acts of Irish terrorism now gave them righteous "cover." Second, it focused and radicalized previously amorphous loyalist opposition in the six northernmost counties of Ireland – Protestant strongholds that one day would comprise Northern Ireland.

In the United States too, intimidation and murder were becoming the means by which radicals settled their internal disputes. In the old Fenian days, secret "councils" would sit in judgment and expel suspected British agents or "traitors." Now they were simply executed. Only a few months before Atkinson and Gladstone met in London, the murder of a troublesome former Clan-na-Gael official, Dr. Patrick Cronin, whose bludgeoned body was found stuffed into a Chicago sewer, marked a turning point for moderate Irish in America – a turning away from radical dream-merchants. The whole business was becoming too bloody and disgraceful.

Cronin's murder exposed the new dark underside of Irish nationalism.

Born in Ireland in 1846 and brought to America as an infant, Cronin's life was a success story similar to that of the Atkinsons – he'd slugged his way into the professional class by dint of education and inner drive. In addition to an M.D., he'd earned a Ph.D. In the early 1880s he settled in Chicago and established a successful medical practice.

Chicago was headquarters for Clan-na-Gael – also

known as the United Brotherhood. This group was founded in the early 1870s and ostensibly modeled on Fenian lines, but it had a smaller national membership (perhaps 10,000) and a harder edge. Instead of circles, the Clan had "camps." An executive board, led by the domineering Chicago lawyer Alexander Sullivan, was firmly in command. Another leading figure in the Clan was someone we've met before: Henri le Caron, still a paid British mole but now a Detroit physician (who had financed his education by moonlighting as a body snatcher[1]).

Soon after joining the Clan – which was considered *de rigeur* for a politically-aware Irish American professional – Cronin began to suspect there were in reality two organizations: a benign public persona, raising funds for Irish peasants and supporting Parnell's Irish parliamentary Bloc; and a clandestine wing directed by Sullivan and a handful of cronies.

The public Clan was an icon of moderation. Sullivan

---

1   Using the alias Dr. Morton, Le Caron was arrested in Toledo in 1878 while engaged in filling an order for 70 bodies for study at the University of Michigan Medical School. Sixty bodies had already been shipped. "Dr. Morton" escaped prior to trial and fled to Chicago.

Body-snatching, though nominally illegal, was not uncommon in the 19th century. Medical schools, desperate for cadavers for anatomical study, secretly enlisted the aid of "resurrectionists" who bribed undertakers or purchased bodies outright.

himself had appointed the redoubtable Rev. Dr. Charles Reilly of Detroit as Treasurer. Father Reilly was Colonel Atkinson's lifelong best friend (the Colonel named a son, Reilly, for him). He and other national figures gave the Clan an imprimatur of mainstream propriety.[1]

In the early 1880's, however, dozens of dynamite bombings in London and Dublin – the so-called Dynamite War – suddenly raised the stakes.[2] Gladstone was in his second

---

1 Father Reilly was Colonel's Atkinson's kind of man: alarmingly bright, aggressive and "ego-centric with a pronounced autocratic streak." Only vaguely interested in the mundane duties of a parish priest, but passionate for the Irish cause, several times Bishop Borgess of Detroit tried to discipline Rev. Reilly for his political activities (which the Church still officially proscribed). But Reilly had the support of other Irish Catholic clergy and promised to fight a suspension all the way to Rome – "with the entire weight of the American Irish hierarchy." Borgess finally backed down.

Of special interest, Father Reilly was one of a handful of priests worldwide to also hold a doctorate – an advanced degree in sacred theology from St. Mary's Seminary in Baltimore. Thus the Rev. *Dr.* Reilly was one of the most visible and trusted Irish personalities in America. His appointment by Sullivan to a high position in Clan-na-ael was masterful.

Reilly's purpose in Ireland in 1889 was to deliver to Parnell $40,000 raised through Clan-na-Gael and the Irish Land League. As it turned out, neither he nor Atkinson ever met with Parnell.

2 More than 60 separate bombings killed at least 100 people.

tenure as the British Prime Minister, and though sympathetic to the Irish nationalist cause he was forced to introduce tough measures to "pacify" Ireland – including a Coercion Act that gave the Viceroy extraordinary latitude to search and arrest without a warrant.

More than two dozen radicals were rounded up and sentenced to long prison terms.

The bombings, a nasty foretaste of IRA tactics a century later, enraged not only the British government but moderate Irish nationalists who were just beginning to see daylight in their long parliamentary quest for self-determination – or at least Home Rule. The home-grown Irish Republican Brotherhood, now backing Parnell's legislative efforts, was so incensed they severed ties with Clan-na-Gael. Investigators suspected that Sullivan and his black-ops crew were financing the "dynamitards," but evidence was scarce and most honest dues-paying American Clan members refused to believe what, after all, were British accusations.

But Cronin would not shut up. By the late 1880s his persistent charge that Sullivan had "embezzled" Clan dues for secret operations – and was continuing to do so – got him banished from a Clan council and permanently silenced.

"The Crime of the Century"

In yet another stroke of irony, the British spy Le Caron was a member of the secret Clan council that ousted Cronin. Several years later, Le Caron testified that Cronin was a "dynamite expert" and up to his elbows in the terrorist plots, but this self-serving charge was never supported by evidence. Available facts argue otherwise.

Let us briefly digress:

Cronin's killing shocked even Chicago, which cherished its reputation as the toughest town in America.[1] Newspapers called it "The Crime of the Century," a short-lived distinction that would be surpassed by the grisly "White City" murders during Chicago's Columbian World Exposition in 1893, not to mention Mayor Carter Harrison's assassination on the last day of the fair.

---

1   More important, this was not a street killing of some "Irish hooligan." It was the methodical liquidation of a respected physician and civic figure. As the story unfolded in the national media, the Cronin case so thoroughly discredited the Irish movement in America that never again would large numbers of ordinary Irish-American citizens lend their monetary support.

Clan-na-Gael had repeatedly denied links to the Dynamite War, but when Sullivan's board called for additional dues to meet undefined "extraordinary expenses" in 1885, some camp leaders around the country protested. They were expelled. Cronin went public.

For years Cronin and Sullivan volleyed accusations through the newspapers. Sullivan dismissed Cronin as a British agent – since Fenian times, the standard label for anyone who disagreed with nationalist policymakers. Cronin claimed Sullivan was in fact the traitor, a "dynamitard ringleader" intent on wrecking the peaceful Home Rule initiatives his organization publicly espoused.

Finally in 1889, the doctor was scheduled to address the Celto-America Society to outline new detailed charges. He disappeared on the night of May 4; the public works department, on May 22, found his decomposing remains wedged into a catch basin at Evanston Avenue and N. 59th Street.

Sullivan was arrested, but released. Again: no evidence. Eventually four men were brought to trial. A leader of local Clan Camp 20 was convicted and received life. But an Irish-American police detective, after 70 hours of deliberation, was acquitted. Juror bribery was suspected and much talked about in the newspapers, not for the first or last time in Chicago.

Protestants had a nickname for Home Rule:
they called it Rome Rule.

Ireland had finally "settled down" into another exhausted lull when in 1886 Gladstone introduced his first Home Rule bill. But it not only split his Liberal party and failed in the House of Commons (by a relatively narrow 343 to 313 vote), a subsequent vote of no-confidence brought down Gladstone's third term as Prime Minister. He was the first of many politicians to be undone by the deadly cross-currents of Irish nationalism – the "curse of Cromwell," as Winston Churchill later put it.

In America, news of the defeat was met with cynicism. But in a speech before the Irish Land League later that year, Colonel Atkinson urged patience. He himself was already a skilled politician, and he understood the English parliamentary process. The battle for Home Rule wasn't finished: this was simply the first round.

Only a small portion of Atkinson's speech survives:

"I know that in many Irish hearts there may be some disappointment at the recent results in England," Atkinson said, "but I know that every thoughtful man will respond gratefully to the work done by Mr. Gladstone... in favor of the great principles of Home Rule."

Gladstone believed in Home Rule on moral grounds, yes, but far more as a practical matter. Irish autonomy was the only way to finally "remove the land issue as a (constant) source of strife," while still preserving Ireland under an Imperial aegis. By this time, however, conservatives and dissident Liberals – later called Liberal Unionists – had congealed into a powerful opposition cadre. One of their leaders was Lord Randolph Churchill (Winston's father), who threatened to play "the Orange card" should Gladstone try again.[1]

---

1   "Orange" refers to the British-backed Protestant elites of Ireland who, although vastly outnumbered by middle-class and poor Catholics, owned the majority of arable land, business and industry. They no longer controlled the ballot box in Ireland but retained sufficient political clout in London (the Orange card) to trump any serious challenge to their security and economic domination. Historically the Orange nickname dates to William III of Orange-Nassau, the Dutch Protestant who with the connivance of Parliament "invaded" England in 1688 and ascended the throne after James II – a Catholic – was deposed. This so-called Glorious Revolution ended any chance of Catholic "sovereignty" being restored in Britain.

Churchill proved good on his threat. Gladstone's second Home Rule Bill in 1893 passed the House of Commons by 43 votes, but was rejected in the House of Lords by one of the largest majorities in history: 419 to 41. With a weary Gladstone now in his 80s and Parnell dead, that vote effectively ended the Home Rule initiative until World War One.

Home Rule was never the holy grail of Irish nationalism: it would still leave Ireland tied to Britain in a federal-style system. But it was a facsimile of nationhood that moderates such as Atkinson could live with – for the time being. Considering the entrenched interests of minority Protestant businessmen and landowners and Tories, it was in truth the best even the most enlightened British government could hope to do.

Though now out of power, the "Grand Old Man" was undeterred. He allied himself with Parnell's solid 80-member Irish parliamentary bloc and was poised for a comeback by 1892. His first order of business would be Home Rule.

It was during this long run-up to Gladstone's remarkable fourth Ministry that he met with Colonel Atkinson, hoping for encouragement from the United States.

"Untold abominations..."

What worried Gladstone – what he pressed Atkinson about – was the prospect of a "capital exodus" from Ireland should Home Rule be enacted. This, of course, was the dire forecast of conservatives. It was a foregone conclusion that a significant percentage of Protestant business and industry would flee a Catholic-governed Ireland. But to fill this void, would the elites of the American-Irish movement (including one Colonel John Atkinson) be prepared to invest heavily in Ireland? Or perhaps even return to the Old Sod to "educate" and lead a new generation of self-governing Irish?

Gladstone asked bluntly: "How do the Americans feel toward Ireland?"[1]

Atkinson assured him: "All parties sympathize with your efforts. Both of the great parties (Democrat and Republican) have expressed their sympathies (for Home Rule) in their platforms."

Gladstone: "Yes... it has been told me that twelve out of every thirteen Americans are with us. But really... how do the *Irish* Americans feel toward us (England)?"

---

1 These remarks are from a long interview with Colonel Atkinson published in the Chicago Tribune, December 30, 1889.

Atkinson: "The Irish-Americans feel differently toward England now from the way they once felt. You have won the hearts of (all) the Irish people... not merely for yourself but for your country."[1]

Gladstone: "I hope so. The Irish have suffered untold abominations at our hands. I believe implicitly in Irish honor and Irish hearts... all they want is justice."

Here we come to a rather disingenuous exchange.

Gladstone leaned in. "Do you think many Irish of means would come back to replace the capital which the Tories allege

---

1   The Colonel did not exaggerate: Gladstone was lionized (at least publicly) by Irish-American leaders. Atkinson himself was among the featured speakers at a Chicago rally in August, 1886, where Gladstone was hailed as "that heroic old man... attempting to burst through the prejudices and barriers of ages." Sharing the podium with Atkinson were Illinois Governor Richard Oglesby, former Speaker of the House Samuel Randall, Irish Land League founder Michael Davitt and... hosting the affair... Alexander Sullivan.

Topic A at the rally was the recent defeat of Gladstone's first Home Rule Bill. William O'Brien, editor of *United Ireland*, quoted to the assembly of 10,000 Parnell's vaguely threatening statement: "... peace and friendship were within the grasp of England if she had been as wise and bold as Mr. Gladstone. And that peace and friendship are within her grasp even yet... upon the day when she once more enthrones Mr. Gladstone in power and commissions him to conclude his treaty of peace with Ireland."

Gladstone would indeed be "enthroned" again, but Parnell would never see Home Rule.

would be withdrawn?" Colonel Atkinson replied, "the Old Land is very dear to the race, and many will return to educate their children… and spend their declining years among their own people."

Gladstone: "I am glad to hear you say so. It has seemed to me that it must be so."

Of course no stenographer was present. These are the Colonel's own polished recollections, given weeks later to a newspaper reporter, from a long rambling conversation that included subjects such as Congressional politics and an arcane ocean-fisheries treaty. But note that Atkinson himself reported using the phrase "declining years."

As the Colonel well understood, no retro-migration to Ireland (in terms of investment capital or homesick descendants) would occur anytime soon. By this time – by the near-turn of the 20th century – the Irish in America had gained a political and social stature far exceeding the dreams of immigrant forebears. Ireland in 1840 had been the most densely populated nation in Europe. By 1920, that demographic was completely reversed. Five million Irish had left the Old Sod. And when their descendants did return – like Atkinson – they were holding round-trip tickets back to America.

Gladstone, as certainly was his purpose, left quite an impression. "His face is familiar to all from pictures," Atkinson said, "but they fail to indicate the intense animation of (Gladstone's) face. He left me with the feeling I had been listening to the voice of one who stands foremost among the statesman of the earth and whose fame will grow as the years roll on." It certainly didn't hurt the Colonel's reputation to say so.

O ROMEO, ROMEO!

"Absconding down a fire escape..."[1]

Colonel Atkinson had barely returned home to Detroit when the political linchpin of the Irish independence movement cracked and gave way. In 1890 the Irish Nationalist Party leader Charles Parnell, admired by Gladstone as "the most remarkable man I have ever met," later described by Prime Minister Herbert Asquith as "one of three or four greatest men of the 19th century," a striking and charismatic figure who one day would be portrayed in a movie by Clark Gable and whom Atkinson openly idolized, was suddenly brought down

---

1   Period cartoon of Parnell making his exit.

by – of all things – an adultery scandal.[1]

---

1   The Colonel had his own liaison in Detroit, which arguably far outshone Parnell's for color and public interest. Atkinson's lover was society damsel Josephine Caspari, daughter of wealthy Michigan lumber baron Stephen Moore and former wife of a notorious Spanish horse breeder.

At Moore's request, Atkinson's law firm had investigated rumors and revealed Max Caspari as a bigamist (another wife in New York, and perhaps a third in Europe). Soon after the divorce and Caspari's eviction from his Fort Street residence, the Colonel became a frequent overnight guest there. But the Spaniard didn't go quietly: one night Caspari broke in and surprised Atkinson and his ex-wife, firing at least one pistol shot into a wall before the Colonel subdued him and sent for police. Another time Caspari confronted Atkinson at his law office, at which point the Colonel beat "that little rat of a Caspari" nearly unconscious.

When one of his business partners in the late 1880s complained to Atkinson – not so much about the Caspari affair itself, but his blatant conduct of it – the Colonel responded blithely that Parnell lived this way, why not him?

Just so.

The Colonel's wife and mother of seven living children, Lida, never publicly complained. When Atkinson died of a heart ailment in Josephine's bed on August 14, 1898, Lida personally arranged for the wake to be held at the Caspari home. Josephine never recovered. She became the "Greta Garbo of Detroit," living as a recluse until her death in the early 1920s. So famous was the "Caspari tragedy" that Henry Ford swooped in to acquire for his collection virtually every piece of furniture or memorabilia at hand in the Caspari residence – unfortunately, no letters. These pieces once comprised

Never mind Clan-na-Gael or the Cronin Case or the Phoenix Murders. It may have been one embittered Irish husband who did more than all the dynamitards to undermine Home Rule for a generation.

The woman in question was Katherine (Katie) O'Shea, the English wife of a prominent member of Parnell's own party, Captain William Henry O'Shea, and niece of a top official in Gladstone's cabinet. Katie and her husband had been living separately since 1875 and in various accounts O'Shea reacted ambivalently to the affair. To preserve his honor he challenged Parnell to a duel in 1881, but others say he encouraged the relationship, hoping to gain political favor from Parnell. Far more economically relevant: the husband stood to gain an inheritance from his wife's aunt. But when the aunt died and O'Shea received nothing, the Captain filed for divorce – naming Parnell as co-respondent.

The suit was filed in late 1889 and the court case unfolded the next year.

By this time Parnell and Mrs. O'Shea had two children together (a third died in infancy) and the relationship was old news amongst England's political elite. Nevertheless, Victorian society was shocked, shocked by the public court proceedings, details

---

a popular exhibit, and are still held in storage at the Henry Ford Museum outside Detroit.

of which were served up gleefully by the London media, most notably *The Times*. As one writer later put it, Parnell was depicted as worse than dishonorable: he was made to look ludicrous.

Withdrawn and sullen, Parnell sat quietly in the courtroom as he was accused of "absconding down a fire escape to avoid Captain O'Shea" and using absurd aliases for trysts with Katie. Here was the man who only a few years earlier had faced down the mighty *London Times*, winning a huge libel settlement after *The Times* used forged letters to implicate him in the Dynamite War. Now he seemed resigned, meek: more focused on his lover's divorce case than any ramifications for Irish nationalism.[1]

---

1   From a legal standpoint, if Parnell had contested the charges (to save his own reputation) this would have complicated and even stymied the court's granting of divorce. In effect, Parnell decided to absorb the full hit in order to hasten Katie's divorce and his eventual marriage to her.

Parnell was known for his "custom of occasionally secluding himself" for long periods (as it turned out, to spend time with Katie). But in December of 1889, shortly after Captain O'Shea filed for divorce, the Irish Nationalist leader "disappeared" for several weeks. This coincided with Colonel Atkinson's and Father Reilly's tour of Ireland and London, and is why they never met Parnell as planned.

Newspapers were full of speculation, and upon the Colonel's disembarkation in America he was besieged for interviews. Under a headline "Parnell Not To Be Found," *The New York Times* on December 4, 1889, said: "Colonel Atkinson discredits rumors

This conduct did not sit well with the Irish clergy, nor the Irish working man. Morality was one thing, but to allow one's self to be publicly mocked and ridiculed by an English barrister: no. He fought to keep control of his party, but one by one and then in great numbers most of Parnell's followers deserted him. Personal feelings aside, Gladstone too was forced to abandon him politically or lose any chance at Home Rule in the future.

As it happened, Parnell's Irish Nationalist party out-lived him under new leadership and the indefatigable Gladstone did succeed in passing Home Rule in the House of Commons in 1893 – only to have it crushed a few weeks later in the House of Lords. By this time affluent "Orange" forces had organized into an immovable barrier, with the help of Parnell's spectacular political and personal self-destruction.

Generations of historians have argued whether Parnell's leadership and influence was already on the wane after the defeat of Home Rule in 1886, but most agree it was the O'Shea scandal that precipitated the "fall of Parnell" and probably Home Rule too. The divorce was granted. Parnell

---

that Mr. Parnell is missing under peculiar circumstances, and says he saw letters written by Mr. Parnell... from a small town where he is resting." How much the Colonel knew is unclear. What is unquestioned is that he remained loyal.

eventually married Katherine O'Shea, but died of heart disease four months later – broken, age 45.

It was good grist for a movie,[1] perhaps, but not for the mill of Irish nationalism. Katie Parnell lived to write a book, but sold it under the name of O'Shea.[2]

---

1   The 1937 film "Parnell" was the biggest box-office flop of Clark Gable's career.

2   Katie Parnell sometimes was derisively referred to as "Kitty," a Victorian slang term for prostitute.

"What fools we were..."

In Atkinson's and Gladstone's day, the concept of Home Rule encompassed *all* of Ireland. The idea of a "two-state solution" – an independent, Catholic-dominated "southern" Ireland and the separate Protestant enclave of Northern Ireland – emerged only slowly. As the political process faltered, as pioneering 19th century moderates died off, and as the specter of Irish terrorism came to the fore, "Orange" opposition coalesced within those six northeastern counties surrounding Ulster, a region with Protestant ancestry dating to the Virgin Queen Elizabeth and Cromwell.

They would leave, they promised, only in coffins.

Rather than physically wrench all of Ireland from the British grasp, it could be argued that terrorism by fanatical splinter groups actually helped *create* Northern Ireland as a separate Unionist state within the British sphere – which it remains today. By 1913 the Ulster Unionist Party and so-called Orange Order had an "army" of 100,000 members ready to fight in the streets if necessary to stop any all-Ireland Home Rule Bill.

As a prelude to negotiations with Irish Republican leaders to create a "free state," in 1920 Parliament formally carved out Northern Ireland to remain British. This was as much a humanitarian move (to avert a certain Protestant-Catholic bloodbath) as a political one.

More than five centuries of subjugation ended in 1922 with establishment of the Irish Free State – excluding those six northern counties. Rather than an independent republic, the Free State was self-governing but nominally tied to Imperial Britain as a dominion similar to Canada. This temporarily satisfied moderates but – of course – not radicals, who viewed anything short of *total* independence of *all* Ireland as a betrayal. What followed was the saddest chapter of all: bitter civil war between factions of Irish Catholics. The pro-treaty Free State forces prevailed, but at a cost that is still being counted by their rival descendants in Irish politics today.

In the early 1920s, as war raged in Ireland, King George V said: "What fools we were not to pass Mr. Gladstone's bill when we had the chance." In 1949, Ireland unilaterally declared itself a Republic.

ILLUMINATIONS

The Fenian mystique

The word "Fenian" was invented in 1858 by founder John O'Mahony. He adapted the term from "Fianna" – a mythological legion of elite Celtic warriors. O'Mahony's entrance exam was far less stringent than in ancient times. Fianna had been required "not to refuse to fight nine men or a nation" and be able to compose soaring lines of verse. Fenian brothers needed only swear an oath. Tens of thousands eventually did.

The original wording set a vaguely paramilitary tone:

"I solemnly pledge my sacred word of honor... that
I will labor with earnest zeal for the liberation of Ireland from
the yoke of England... and that I will implicitly obey the
commands of my superior officers in the Fenian Brotherhood."

Borrowing from the Fianna mystique, O'Mahony's oath included a requirement that all brothers "...promote feelings of love, harmony and kindly forebearance (sic) among Irishmen." This passage is a key to understanding Fenian ethics. Although today O'Mahony's organization would probably be listed on world terrorist bulletins, to the Fenians of the 1860s chivalry still mattered. Even Canadian officers (grudgingly) commented on their unfailing manners in the midst of the 1866 invasion.

In his *History of the Fenian Raid*, a Canadian militia officer, George Denison, wrote:

"(The Fenians) have been called plunderers... marauders, yet no matter how unwilling we may be to admit it, the positive fact remains that they stole but few valuables, that they destroyed, comparatively speaking, little or nothing, and that they committed no outrages on the inhabitants (of Fort Erie), but treated everyone with courtesy and respect."

With the failure of the Canadian schemes and swift demise of the American Fenian movement in the 1870s, that "courtesy and respect," as we have seen in Part Six of this narrative, gave way to indiscriminate bombings and political assassination – tactics the Civil War-veteran Fenians would never have countenanced.

A *"thousand mile front"*

The elaborate and overwrought 1866 Fenian invasion plan was the work of "Fighting" General Tom Sweeny, a well-respected veteran of the Shiloh and Atlanta campaigns. He envisioned a "thousand mile front," with key mobilization points stretching from Chicago to Vermont, and multiple landings to overwhelm the slim resources of provincial forces. The plan eventually called for roughly 50,000 Fenian soldiers arriving at various start points from 22 states (including former Confederate states), over an unreliable transportation grid of rail, river, and horse-drawn coach.

Only 5,000 to 7,000 Fenians ever reached their designated start points – most of these long after O'Neill had crossed on June 1, 1866, and the possibility of resupply and reinforcement had been cut off.

Scapa Flow, 1914:

a measure of Fenian revenge on the Royal Navy

If necessity is the mother of invention, Irish hatred of the British might be a distant relative – at least in the case of one technological breakthrough. The first "modern submarine" was commissioned and underwritten by the Fenian movement. Irish inventor John Holland designed and built his "Ram" in 1881 for the express purpose of sinking British warships and commercial vessels.

Unlike earlier concepts such as the CSS Hunley, which sank three times and claimed 32 sailors before the Confederacy finally gave up on it, Holland's design did not rely entirely on ballast for submersion: it maintained a controllable degree of buoyancy and employed fins and planes for diving. But his truly pioneering innovation was an eleven-foot-long pneumatic "gun" that could be loaded (and reloaded) *internally*. As today, torpedoes were fired from a watertight compartment in the bow.

During secret sea trials the 19-ton prototype Fenian Ram was able to submerge to 60 feet and its three-man crew fired several dummy projectiles. More important, the Ram success-fully resurfaced. Holland's design worked. But as the reader of this narrative will find unsurprising, disputes within Fenian leadership over financing ($23,000) and plans for this wonder weapon scuttled the entire project.

The frustrated Holland finally took his concept to the United States Navy, which adopted one of his later designs as SS-1 in 1898. That basic design was studied and improved on by naval engineers in Europe – particularly in Germany.

Although he died in 1914, Holland did live long enough to see his concept in action against the British. With the outbreak of World War One the German U-Boat fleet was still modeled on Holland's principles. In a daring raid on the Grand Fleet's anchorage at Scapa Flow, a single German U-boat slipped into harbor and sank three cruisers – the most lopsided Royal Navy loss to this day.

A copy of the Fenian Ram survives and is on display at the Paterson Museum in New Jersey.

The Church v. The Fenians

The supreme irony of the American Irish-Catholic Fenian movement was that its strongest opponent was neither the British or Canadians – but the Catholic Church.

With the exception of a few renegade parishes in Ireland and America, Fenianism was condemned from Catholic pulpits. Ultimately, in January of 1870, a Supreme Tribunal in Rome formally "excommunicated" the Brotherhood and by extension any member engaged in "seditious" action. For the vast majority of Fenians, who were devout practicing Catholics, this meant British bullets were only a minor temporal risk compared to eternal damnation. (The threat of excommunication undoubtedly had a damping effect on turnout for O'Neill's "second invasion" in May of that year.)

Why would the Church oppose an organization whose stated purpose was the "emancipation" of oppressed Catholics? Various bishops expended reams of high-minded prose arguing their position. The gist of it was expressed in the *American Catholic Quarterly*: "We would all like to see dear old Catholic Ireland get her full rights of civil and religious freedom... but we must do no evil so that good may come of it."

Right. But most parishioners – including Fenians – understood that politics and self-interest played an equally significant role.

To begin with, most Catholic leaders saw the Fenians as just one more "secret society" of hooligans – like the Molly Maguires – who would bring not Irish liberation but more bloodshed and British retribution. Since the Cromwell era the Vatican had maintained a fragile arrangement with England. Catholic churches and schools were permitted in Ireland, as long as Catholics didn't threaten the status quo of minority Protestant domination. The Catholic clergy preferred to keep their little wooden churches and subservient status – i.e., "registering" and tithing to Protestant authorities – rather than risk everything once a generation by backing yet another failed revolt. One can see the point. Not once in more than two centuries had an armed rebellion produced anything except deceased Catholic parishioners.

It was difficult enough for Irish bishops and priests to see their beloved churches — as D'Arcy put it — systematically depopulated by famine and immigration. Fenianism only threatened to up-end the Church's precarious existence in Ireland.

In the United States these concerns went deeper. Here the Church was trying to establish itself in a far more permissive yet still Protestant-dominated environment. Except for a handful of individual priests, Catholic clergy in America were hostile to the taking of Fenian oaths and collection of weekly dues from relatively poor immigrant Irish parishioners. They saw the Brotherhood as a gang of charlatans preying on the sentiments of gullible immigrants. Those dues would be better spent building new churches and educating Catholic children rather than chasing old delusions.

Reading through correspondence of the Church hierarchy at this time, one is struck by the patronizing attitude toward Irish immigrant parishioners who are frequently characterized as "weak-minded" and easily misled.

We must also remember, too, that the Church had global priorities. In some respects, strife in Ireland was a wag-the-dog phenomenon for the Vatican. Getting along with England was essential to the success of far-flung missionary operations around the world, a world largely dominated by Britain in the 19th century. And so in sermons condemning Fenianism, the government of Great Britain often is referred to as the "legitimate" authority in Ireland.

Fenian leaders naturally dismissed the Church's objections out of hand.

The "secret society" accusation they found laughable – and the reader may well agree. With the exception of O'Neill's war plans for 1870, there was nothing secret about Fenianism in North America. Leaders held press conferences and clearly outlined their goals. Members paraded down the main streets of major cities. The Fenians loudly and repeatedly declared themselves "at war with the oligarchy of Great Britain."

More difficult to defend were Fenian leaders' continuous calls for special donations to "invasion funds." Even a jaundiced non-Catholic observer such as Pinkerton was dismayed by the way Chicago's Fenian circles – which contributed next to nothing in terms of men or material toward the 1866 and 1870 invasions of Canada – had thoroughly "drained the resources" of local Fenian supporters.

"Not admissible to the sacraments of the Church"

The Fenians' ongoing battle with the Church was distilled in the personal experience of one intellectually-gifted but emotionally-conflicted Irish American priest, Rev. John McMullen.

In the summer of 1865, at the end of Civil War, McMullen was a leading young figure in Chicago's burgeoning archdiocese. Many believed he was on the fast track toward becoming its next Archbishop.[1] But that August, an incident in St. Paul, Minnesota, prompted McMullen to open an ecclesiastical dialogue on the thorny problems of Fenianism. McMullen's essay, published after his death, undoubtedly served as fodder for numerous Sunday sermons.

For most Irish American priests and bishops, the Fenian question was purely theological. But for McMullen it was also personal.

What triggered his self-searching in 1865 was this:

Leaders of the Fenian circle in St. Paul were planning

---

1   McMullen eventually became the first Bishop of Davenport and founder of St. Ambrose College. His life and career are part of a longer work on the Atkinson and McMullen families.

elaborate funeral services for a deceased member at St. Patrick's Church, to include a colorful "pageant" and eulogies by prominent Fenians. When the news of this reached archdiocesan offices in St. Louis, which was then the governing See for Minnesota, Archbishop Kenrick laid down the liturgical law. Not only did he forbid religious services for Fenians at St. Patrick's (or any other Catholic church), he forbade entry to Calvary Cemetery for anyone "bearing the insignia of Fenianism."

In a brief but scathing letter printed in the *St. Louis Republican*, the archbishop reminded all good Catholics that "members of the Fenian Brotherhood... are not admissible to the sacraments of the Church as long as they are united with that association... which I have long considered immoral in its object – the exciting of rebellion in Ireland – and unlawful in its means while at peace with England."

All of this reached a deep place in McMullen:

One year earlier, in the summer of 1864, Father McMullen himself had delivered the tearful eulogy in Chicago for a genuine lion of the Union cause, brevet Brigadier General James Mulligan – McMullen's best friend, a fellow Irishman, and an avowed Fenian (which McMullen surely knew at the time).

Mulligan and McMullen were star pupils and classmates in the 1850s at Chicago's first Catholic university, St. Mary's of the Lake on the south side. At first they were intellectual rivals, but soon inseparable friends. McMullen chose a career in the Church (and was sent to Rome for seminary studies). Mulligan chose the law. He was admitted to the Chicago bar in 1856, two years before McMullen was ordained.

In the pre-Civil War years the two remained very close in Chicago. Mulligan helped to edit a number of regional Catholic newspapers – such as the *Western Tablet* – to which McMullen contributed articles on issues of the day. When comparing McMullen's later writing with prose from these early years, a careful reader can see Mulligan's editorial hand. The young priest was a good writer, but Mulligan gave his articles much tighter syntax, clarity and a more polished tone. Mulligan must have been a fine lawyer.

When the war broke out, Mulligan organized and commanded the 23rd Illinois Volunteer Infantry Regiment known as the "Irish Brigade" – not to be confused with the New York regiment by the same name. Described in newspaper accounts as "over six feet" with a "muscular frame" and a "frank Celtic face," Mulligan was a "dashing" figure with a war record to match. Fort Mulligan in West Virginia was named for him, and his Irish Brigade engaged in a number of savage battles from Missouri to the Shenandoah Valley.

Mulligan was killed at the Second Battle of Kernstown, near Winchester, Virginia, and the manner of his death was the stuff of John O'Neill's dreams. While standing high in the saddle to rally his troops, Mulligan was mortally wounded by a Confederate sharpshooter. As officers tried to carry him from the field he ordered: "Lay me down, boys... and save the flag." He died in Confederate custody two days later.

We can imagine the impact on McMullen, and how little his friend's proscribed Fenian membership must have mattered to the priest. The reader is reminded that Mulligan died in 1864, long before Fenian leadership had decided on "the Canada scheme." We can only wonder what decisive role Mulligan might have played – if any.

This background may explain why in his comments on Fenianism, unlike most priests and bishops of the time, McMullen was extraordinarily lenient on the "faithful" who had strayed into the dreamscape of Irish liberation. By the same token he was unsparing in his condemnation of those leaders who played on Irish Catholic "ignorance" of what constitutes "secret societyism."

McMullen wrote: "As men are most easily deceived in matters touching their fondest attachments, it is not remarkable that the Irish people should frequently be deluded by visionary projects for the amelioration of the condition of their native land. There were honest, true, brave men in the Fenian Brotherhood (read James Mulligan)... but also timeservers, vain enthusiastic creatures, even imposters whose purpose was to enrich themselves. It would be unfair to fix the stigma of dishonesty on poor, simple, upright, patriotic people who gave their means, who love Ireland... and imagined that the hour of her redemption was at hand."

A page from Madison's 1812 playbook

The idea of seizing Canadian territory to use as a "bargaining chip" against the British did not originate with the Fenians – this was precisely Madison's goal in the War of 1812. Sweeny and O'Neill's plans of attack in 1866 and 1870 were almost identical to Madison's strategies. But as with the Fenians 40 years later, in 1812 what "saved Canada for England" was a combination of military unpreparedness, logistical incompetence and – let's face it – a failure of nerve.

It is not our intention to refight The War of 1812 here, but parallels with the Fenian invasions are so uncanny as to warrant this sidebar.

Basically the war was unfinished business from the Revolution. Some referred to it as a "Second War of Independence." Unable to defeat the colonists on the ground, for decades the British showed no respect for American rights at sea. Royal Navy ships routinely stopped American commercial vessels, seized cargos and "impressed" sailors into British servitude.

This bullying extended to America's poorly defined northern and northwestern borders with Canada where

British agents enjoyed meddling in Indian affairs. They forged alliances, sold arms to hostile tribes, and occasionally led raids on American settlements. By 1812, the "war hawks" in Congress and President James Madison had had enough.

Like the Fenians in 1866, America confidently declared war on Britain – and promptly bungled it.

Lacking a serious navy, Madison staked everything on the stunning conquest of lightly-defended Canada. Although the American army in 1812 numbered less than 12,000 men, he believed volunteer militia could win the day, as they had a generation before. Attacks would come from the frontier outpost of Detroit and the Niagara peninsula. (Sound familiar?) Madison's Secretary of State James Monroe was so enthused by the prospect of an easy victory he had to be talked out of assuming a field command.

England in 1812 was preoccupied, to say the least, with Napoleon Bonaparte.[1] Only a handful of British brigades were stationed in what was left of the North American colonies – and it was assumed these were the junior varsity, England needing its best soldiers on the continent. Once a few feisty American militia units were entrenched upon Canadian soil,

---

1   To stay neutral, America had stopped trading with France and England. This Non-Intercourse Act infuriated the British, who increased their harassment of American shipping.

the British would immediately come to terms. This was the thinking. As mentioned earlier, Madison's predecessor Jefferson had openly opined that taking Ontario would be "a mere matter of marching."

But it turned out those few redcoats in Canada were more than a match for what America could throw at them.

On July 12, 1812, an army of 2,000 militiamen under Michigan's 60-year old territorial governor William Hull crossed into Canada from Detroit – but their battle plans were already compromised. A few days earlier a British patrol on Lake Erie intercepted Hull's supply ship containing detailed maps of his intended attack on Fort Amherstburg: that option was now eliminated. Then Hull learned that an apparently large British force had captured Fort Mackinac without firing a shot... and was turning south to confront him. What panicked him was an intelligence report (actually a British ruse) that many thousands of scalp-seeking[2] warriors – an Indian confederation under the Shawnee leader Tecumseh – were now armed and in league with the British.

---

2   The British practice of paying "scalp bounties" to their Indian allies began during the French and Indian War and persisted through the War of 1812. Whether or not Tecumseh's confederation was being paid by the scalp, this vengeful prospect terrified most Americans. In Hull's case, he surrendered to the first white face he saw.

Hull withdrew back to Fort Detroit and urgently requested reinforcements. When the British showed up a few days later with 1,200 men (and only 400 warriors), Hull surrendered without a fight.[1] Detroit remained in British hands until 1815.

The Niagara campaign was equally disastrous. The same (extraordinary) British commander who'd outfoxed Hull in Detroit quickly marched east to meet American regulars and militia crossing from Lewistown, New York. At the Battle of Queenston Heights – not far from Niagara Falls on the Canadian side – an American force of roughly 3,000 under Major General Stephen Van Rensselaer was crushed by Sir Issac Brock's brigades.[2] Nearly 1,000 prisoners were taken. Even more humiliating, some of Rensselaer's militia had refused to cross.

So much for a military cake-walk in Canada. As the Fenians would learn.

---

1 Hull was court-martialed, found guilty of cowardice and sentenced to be shot. He was reprieved by Madison and spent the remainder of his life in Massachusetts – writing books to clear his name.

2 Brock's deserved knighthood was posthumous. He was killed in action at Queenston Heights. Today monuments to Brock are not hard to find. He is considered the "savior of Canada."

The case of the preoccupied pilot: how to
disable a 600-ton warship blocking your way to Canada

If not for an inspired piece of Fenian subterfuge, O'Neill's 1866 invasion of Canada – via the treacherous Niagara River, beginning shortly after midnight on June 1 – probably would have gotten no farther than Pratt's Iron Works wharf near Buffalo. Even the victim of this skullduggery, Captain Andrew Bryson of the *USS Michigan*, privately admitted it was a stroke of genius.

By the evening of May 31, the long-rumored Fenian crossing appeared imminent as hundreds of Irish men – perhaps 2,000 – gathered on commercial docks near Black Rock, five miles north of Buffalo. Lacking any directives from Washington, local authorities reacted on gut instinct and initiative. Buffalo's district attorney, for example, wired terse warnings to officials in Hamilton and Toronto, but thus far the Irish had broken no laws and he could only watch and wait.

The district attorney's next telegraph was to the commander of the formidable *USS Michigan*, the Navy's first iron-hulled warship, anchored off Buffalo. Only a few days earlier the patrolling *Michigan* had seized a shipment of Fenian gunpowder on Lake Erie. Now she was the only military obstacle between the Irish and a lodgment on Canadian soil. As a precaution Captain Bryson had ordered his boilers fired up and prepared to make steam. Cannon were loaded.

The mere sight of the 600-ton *Michigan* suddenly coming alongside O'Neill's rickety canal boats and barges – or, say, a single howitzer blast across their bows in the pre-dawn darkness – probably would have been sufficient to dissuade most Fenian volunteers. But the vessel was in effect completely disabled. Bryson's pilot and second assistant engineer – both Irish-Americans – were mysteriously AWOL.

Bryson was a new commander, having arrived in April. He (and the Fenians) well understood that any attempt to navigate or maneuver on the notorious Niagara at night without an experienced pilot would invite disaster. So as he read the D.A.'s urgent telegram, Bryson could only pace the deck of the *Michigan's* bridge and stare ashore – as O'Neill's men crossed unmolested throughout the night.

Not until nearly five in the morning did the pilot, Patrick Murphy, reappear on the decks of the *Michigan* – chastened and thoroughly inebriated. The captain immediately placed him under arrest by Marines stationed on board. But even though Murphy could hardly navigate his own person at this point, Bryson had little choice but to give him the helm and steam post-haste for Black Rock. An hour later the *Michigan* somehow arrived, but 20 minutes after another Fenian supply barge had departed for Canada.

For obvious reasons this embarrassing debacle was never mentioned publicly, and thus has been overlooked by generations of historians. (It was uncovered by Bradley Rogers in his excellent history of the *Michigan*. Rogers had access to captain's logs and private reports to Secretary of the Navy Gideon Welles.) The *Michigan* was later praised for her role in intercepting further reinforcements and then capturing O'Neill and the main body of Fenians as they attempted to cross back to Buffalo. But most Canadian authorities remained bitter over Bryson's tardy initial response – never knowing the real reason why.

It turned out that engineer James P. Kelly was an ardent Fenian sympathizer, if not a card-carrying member. In the run-up to the June 1 invasion, Fenians leaders knew the *Michigan* could prove troublesome. Kelly was recruited to entice Murphy – easily done, as it happened – into a raucous night on the town, complete with an open bar tab and the favors of "a lady friend," all generously underwritten by the Fenian Brotherhood.

(*Above*) A company of Victoria Rifles on parade in Montreal after the failed Fenian invasion of 1866. (*Below left*) Monument in Queen's Park, Toronto, commemorating militia volunteers who died at the Battle of Ridgeway, 1866. (*Below right*) Canadian General Service Medal, Fenian Raid 1870.

Plate 1

(Above) Thomas D'Arcy McGee, Canadian politician and "Father of Confederation."

Irish-born and Catholic-raised, McGee became a prominent writer and organizer of the 1848 Young Ireland movement. But unlike William Smith O'Brien, he managed to escape arrest and flee to America. For nearly a decade he continued writing and speaking out as an avowed Irish nationalist before moving to Canada in 1857.

Once in Canada, McGee's views began to moderate sharply. And when it became clear the Fenians intended to militarily conquer his adopted homeland, McGee reversed philosophical course and denounced the brotherhood as a "seditious society" whose name was derived from "Pagan darkness." In the aftermath of Ridgeway it was McGee – now an elected minister – who spurred confederation of the most populous Canadian provinces: their first step toward nationhood.

McGee was shot to death in 1868 by an alleged Canadian Fenian sympathizer. At this writing, he is still the only federal Canadian official ever to have been assassinated in office. Although Fenians regarded McGee as a traitor, his convicted assassin was not a member of the brotherhood and no conspiratorial link was ever established.

(Above right) The funeral of D'Arcy McGee.

Plate 2

(Above left) Gilbert McMicken, Canadian politician, magistrate and spymaster.

Like all Canadian leaders, McMicken consistently strove to maintain neutrality and deprive the Americans any excuse for casting an untoward eye northward. But with Canada's porous frontier border and slender military resources, this proved impossible. During the Civil War, McMicken's detectives were only partially effective against Confederate agents attempting to use Canada as a military base. In 1864 a company of Confederates launched a raid from Canada into Vermont, an event that stoked anti-Canadian feeling for years afterward and helped fuel Fenian ambitions.

After the war, McMicken turned his spy network toward the Fenian Brotherhood, which made no secret of its plan to hoist the flag of Irish liberation in British North America. Despite solid intelligence (via Major Le Caron) and repeated warnings from McMicken, the 1866 invasion caught most Canadian leaders by surprise.

(Above right) Thomas Miller Beach (Major Henri Le Caron), British raconteur, Union officer, presumed Fenian leader, confidant of O'Neill, convicted body snatcher, physician and spy. Miller's peripatetic life has been the subject of at least one book and a possible movie. As an agent for the British, he spent two decades spying on Fenian activities from within the highest echelons of power – yet was never suspected until his sudden appearance at Parnell's libel trial in London.

Plate 3

(Above) Fenian General John O'Neill, the "man of action" who led a Fenian rout of British forces in Ontario. His short-lived victory at the Battle of Ridgeway catapulted O'Neill from a modest regimental role in a Tennessee Fenian circle to international fame.

(Above right) Ulysses S. Grant. Unlike his predecessor as president, Grant acted quickly to halt the Fenians' second invasion of Canada in 1870. On May 24 he issued a stern proclamation threatening arrest for any violators of Canadian-U.S. neutrality, and dispatched U.S. Marshal George Foster to confront O'Neill at his camp in northern Vermont. O'Neill brusquely dismissed Foster, who had no supporting troops, but the confrontation seemed to have rattled the Fenian commander (who had expected no interference from the government).

Later that day, rather than wait for the promised but slow-arriving Fenian regiments from New England circles – and unaware that Colonel William Atkinson had already reached nearby Malone, New York, with more than 1,500 eager Midwestern and ex-Confederate volunteers – O'Neill mounted a hasty and narrow border attack on Eccles Hill (with a few hundred troops) that was easily thrown back by well-positioned Canadian militia.

As the Fenians retreated in disorder back across the border, Foster found and arrested O'Neill. Just that quickly, the grandiose vision evaporated. A second improvised and under-strength Fenian incursion did reach Huntingdon, but it was driven back by Canadian cavalry.

Plate 4

(Above) The Colonel rides to the rescue (sort of): By all accounts an accomplished horseman, Colonel John Atkinson is pictured here at his estate on Bois Blanc island, circa 1880. At one point Atkinson and business partner (later bitter rival) James Randall owned virtually all of what today is better known as Bob-Lo Island, near the mouth of the Detroit River. Atkinson also briefly owned a resort home (now on the National Register of Historic Places) on Mackinac Island.

But Michigan wasn't the only place where the Colonel speculated in real estate...

In 1877 the appearance of Atkinson on "a big black stallion no one else could handle" electrified the disheartened Irish settlers of north-central Nebraska. Atkinson had purchased land to support O'Neill's troubled "Irish colonies" scheme, but when he arrived from Detroit to survey his new Nebraska town he found, again, the perils of a joint venture with O'Neill. His sixty acres of "buffalo wallows" proved untenable for any kind of permanent construction.

Irish settlers across the Elkhorn River, however, did succeed in building a town – and named it Atkinson in the Colonel's honor.

Plate 5

(Above) Detail from map of Nebraska, 1895. The town of O'Neill was founded by the Fenian leader as a utopian "Irish colony" – where poor Irish immigrants could escape the slums and day-wage slavery of Eastern cities. But greenhorn Irish settlers struggled until Custer's 1874 expedition confirmed gold in the Black Hills, transforming O'Neill into a prosperous way station and depot. A second colony was named for Colonel John Atkinson (see previous page).

(Above) Newspaper ad for the practice of Dr. Henri Le Caron, who managed to find time away from his Fenian spying activities to earn degrees from Detroit College of Medicine and Rush Medical College. An historical irony: in the column at left, an announcement of a town hall lecture by John O'Neill entitled "The late Fenian Invasion of Canada, and why it failed."

Plate 6

The first "modern submarine" was commissioned and underwritten by the Fenian movement. Irish inventor John Holland designed and built his "Ram" in 1881 for the express purpose of sinking British warships and commercial vessels. Disputes within Fenian leadership over financing ($23,000) and plans for this wonder weapon scuttled the entire project. The frustrated Holland finally took his concept to the United States Navy and the Holland Torpedo Boat Company would eventually become General Dyanmics, one of the world's largest defense contractors.

JOHN P. HOLLAND
"FATHER OF THE MODERN SUBMARINE"
BORN LISCANNOR, IRELAND 1841
DIED NEW JERSEY, USA 1914
DESIGNER OF THE U.S. NAVY'S FIRST SUBMARINE
USS HOLLAND (SS I)

Plate 7

(Above) William Gladstone, 1809 – 1898, four-time Prime Minister, high-minded Liberal and tireless exponent of Irish Home Rule, which would have established self-government (if not full independence) for all of Ireland. For many Irish-Americans, particularly the Atkinsons and other moderates, Gladstone represented the first real conscience in Britain and a realistic hope for some measure of autonomy in Ireland after centuries of subjugation and conflict.

Gladstone forged a parliamentary alliance with the remnants of Charles Parnell's bloc of Irish M.P.s and eventually succeeded in pushing a Home Rule Bill through the contentious House of Commons – only to see it stopped by entrenched monied interests in the House of Lords.

Plate 8

"GOOD HEALTH!"

(Above) Cartoon by John Porter, *The Weekly Freeman*, 28 December 1889, entitled: "Good health and success to both of you, say millions of Men all over the World". The illustrated reference to Hawarden is Gladstone's home in Flintshire, England, where Parnell visited in December 1889 to discuss Home Rule for Ireland.

(Right)
Colonel John Atkinson about the time he met with Gladstone.

Plate 9

(Above) Charles Stewart Parnell, 1846 – 1891, considered the greatest Irish statesman of the 19th century. He was brought down – and with him, some scholars believe, any prospects for Home Rule in the late 19th century – by a petty adultery scandal.

(Right) Parnell's paramour Katherine O'Shea, wife of an Irish supporter and the niece of a member of Gladstone's cabinet.

Plate 10

(Above left) Irish nationalist and suspected terrorist-financier Alexander Sullivan of Chicago's Clan-na-Gael. *(Above right)* Dr. Patrick Cronin.

By the 1880's, with the military aspirations of Fenianism now completely discredited, the cause of Irish independence took a darker turn. One controversial group headquartered in Chicago, Clan-na-Gael, was suspected of secretly financing the so-called Dynamite War of bombings and assassinations in London and Dublin.

When one notable Clan-na-Gael member, Dr. Patrick Cronin, publicly accused clan leaders of "embezzling" honest dues for black operations, he was found murdered – his body stuffed into a Chicago sewer.

The rise of Irish terrorism did much to undermine the efforts of converted moderates such as the Atkinsons, and to drive a wedge between Gladstone's fragile political alliances aimed at Home Rule. In fact, Irish Republican radicals wanted no part of Home Rule – for them it was independence or else. Moreover, terrorism stiffened the resolve of militant Ulster-based Protestant groups such as the Orange Order and Unionist Party.

As a result, by the early 20th century independence for all of Ireland was no longer a political possibility under any circumstances. Before agreeing on negotiations to create the predominately Catholic Irish Free State, the government in London took steps to ensure the six Protestant-majority northern counties would always remain nominally British (under British protection).

Thus the two Irelands we know today.

Plate 11

Lord Randolph Churchill *(above)* helped engineer defeat of Irish Home
Rule in 1893. But a generation later his son Winston *(below)*, as British
Colonial Secretary, negotiated creation of the Irish Free State.

Plate 12

Bibliography

PRIMARY, SECONDARY AND GENERAL REFERENCE SOURCES

American Annual Cyclopedia and Register of Important Events, 1865
(Appleton & Co.)

Annual Report to the Secretary of War, 1868

Atlantic Monthly, Making of America Project, 1905

Autobiography of William Henry Seward (Appleton & Co., 1891)

Before Today: A History of Holt County, Nebraska, Nellie Snyder
Yost (Miles Publishing Co., 1976)

Burton Historical Collection, Detroit Public Library, Detroit,
Michigan

Call in Pinkerton's: American Detectives at Work for Canada, David
Ricardo Williams (Dundurn Press, 1998)

Chicago Public Library

Civil War Years: Canada and the United States, Robin W. Winks
(McGill-Queen's Press, 1998)

England's Irish Slaves, Robert E. West (American Ireland Education
Foundation, Stony Point, NY)

Fenian Brotherhood: A Few Useful Hints to Irishmen, and
SomeValuable Information for Americans, Concerning
Ireland, by "an Irishman" (Dakin, Davies & Metcalf, 1864)

Fenian Raid of '66, Buffalo Historical Society, 1921

Fenianism in North America, W. S. Niedhardt (The Pennsylvania
State University Press, 1975)

Fort Erie Historical Society, Ridgeway, Ontario (Canada)

Give Your Other Vote To The Sister, Debbie Marshall (U. of
Calgary Press)

Greater Britain: A Record of Travel in English-Speaking
Countries During 1866 and 1867, Charles Wentworth
Dilke (Harper & Brothers, 1869)

Guardian of the Great Lakes, Bradley Rodgers (University of
Michigan Press, 1996)

History and Biographical Gazetteer of Montreal to Year 1892, John
Douglas Borthwick (Lovell, 1892)

History of Detroit and Michigan, Silas Farmer (Farmer & Co.,
1889)

History of Sarnia to 1900, George and Leslie K. Smith (St. Clair
County Public Library)

History of the English-Speaking Peoples (Volume One), Winston
    Churchill (Dodd Mead, 1965)

History of the Fenian Raid on Fort Erie, Major George Denison,
    Toronto, 1866

Irish-American Units in the Civil War, Thomas G. Rodgers
    (Osprey Publishing, 2008)

*Irish Military Service during the American Civil War: A Case Against
    Assimilation* (Abstract), Michelle L. Hartman

Irish Nationalism and The American Contribution, Lawrence J.
    McCaffrey, editor (Ayer Publishing)

Irish Rebel: John Devoy, Terry Golway (Macmillan, 1988)

Lambton County Library, Wyoming, Ontario (Canada)

Love Song to the Plains, Mari Sandoz (University of Nebraska
    Press, 1961)

Narrative of the Fenian Invasion of Canada, Alexander Somerville
    (Lawson & Co., 1866)

Nebraska, Its Advantages, Resources and Drawbacks, Edwin A Curley
    (The American News Company, 1876)

Papers Relating to the Treaty of Washington, 1872

Pioneer Collections, Michigan State Historical Society

Port Huron: Celebrating Our Past 1857-2007 (Sight Creative, 2006)

Proceedings of the Second National Congress of the Fenian Brotherhood, Cincinnati, Ohio, January 1865

Report of General John O'Neill, President of the Fenian Brotherhood: On the Attempt to Invade Canada, May 25th 1870 (New York Public Library)

Sarnia Observer, Sarnia, Ontario, Canada (Archives)

Secret History of the Fenian Conspiracy: Its Origin, Objects & Ramifications, John Rutherford (Kegan Paul & Co., London, 1877)

Sessional Papers, Canada Parliament, 1872

St. Clair County, Michigan, Its History and Its People, William Lee Jenks (Lewis, 1912)

St. Clair County Public Library, Port Huron, Michigan

Strange Empire: A Narrative of the Northwest, Joseph Kinsey Howard (Minnesota Historical Society Press, 1994)

Summer Dreams, the Story of Bob-Lo Island, Patrick Livingston (Wayne State University Press, Detroit, 2008)

The Fenian Movement in the United States: 1858-1886, William
   D'Arcy (The Catholic University of America Press, 1947)

The Great Shame, Thomas Keneally (Serpentine Publishing Co.,
   1998)

The Green Flag in America, Thomas Fleming, American Heritage,
   June 1979

The Last Invasion of Canada, Hereward Senior, Canadian War
   Museum, Dundurn Press, 1991

The Nation, October 19, 1871

Troublous Times in Canada, A History of the Fenian Raids of 1866
   and 1870, John A. MacDonald (reprinted by BiblioBazaar,
   2007)

Twenty-Five Years in the Secret Service: The Recollections of a
   Spy, Major Henri Le Caron, aka Thomas Miller
   Beach (Heinemann, London, 1892)

William Smith O'Brien and the Young Ireland Rebellion of 1848,
   Robert Sloan (Four Courts Press, 2000)

Index

3rd Michigan Infantry, 11, 13, 64

5th Indiana Cavalry, 67

13th Fenian Tennessee regiment, 69

22nd Michigan, 11-12

    Company C, 12

Acheson name, 29

Act of Settlement, 34

Act of Union, 40

Aetna Insurance, 90

Alabama, CSS, 55-56

    "Alabama Claims", 56, 60, 73, 84,
      106

American Catholic Quarterly, 154

Amherstburg, Ontario, 52, 165

Andersonville Prison, Georgia, 12

Ascendancy, The, 35

Asquith, Prime Minister Herbert, 137

Atkinson Avenue, 14, 87

Atkinson Brothers, 11, 14, 23-24, 31,
    47-48, 50, 88, 90, 104, 116, 123

Atkinson, Colonel John, 13-14, 23,
    38, 48, 67, 82, 86, 112, 115-116,
    121-122, 124, 126, 130, 132,
    133-135, 137-138, 140, 143

Atkinson Elementary School, 14

Atkinson, James, 14

Atkinson, James (Sr.) and Elizabeth,
    21, 31, 38

Atkinson name, 29-31, 38, 158

Atkinson, Nebraska, 111, 116

Atkinson, O'Brien, 14, 20, 23, 59, 86

Atkinson Park, 14

Atkinson, Patrick, 12

Atkinson-Port Huron "Circle", 21,
    23, 47, 81

Atkinson, William F., 3-4, 11, 14, 17,
    23, 48, 71, 81, 86, 88, 92, 96-99,
    100-103, 105-107, 115

Bay City, Michigan, 22, 82, 95

Bitney, Frank, 116

Borgess, Bishop of Detroit, 126

Bragg, General Braxton, 13

British North America, 3-4

Brock, Sir Issac, "Savior of Canada",
    166

Buffalo, New York, 3

Burlington, Vermont, 105

Campobello Island, New Brunswick,
    69-70, 78

Canadian Confederation, 71, 112

Caron Le, Henri, *see Le Caron*

Caspari, Josephine, 138

Caspari, Max, 138

Catholic Emancipation, 40

Charles I, 33

Chattanooga, Battle of, 12

Chicago, Illinois, 15, 17-18, 22, 47, 50-51, 124-125, 151, 160

    Archdiocese of Chicago, 158

    Chicago Bar, 160

    Chicago's Columbian World Exposition of 1893, 128

    "Crime of the Century", 128

    Fenian Calvary, 66

    Fenian Circles, 63, 157

    Fenian Parade on Wabash Avenue, 78

    First Catholic university, 159

    Chicago Tribune, 122

    Clan-na-Gael Headquarters, 124

    Fenian Rally of 1866, 77

    Funeral of Gen. James Mulligan, 159

    Great Chicago Fire, 22

    Irish National Fair, 58

    Juror bribery, 129

    Metropolitan Hall, 58

    Rally of 1886, 134

    Republican Fenian Club, 50

Chickamauga, Battle of, 12, 13, 68

Churchill, Lord Randolph, 131

Churchill, Winston, 41, 130-131

Clan-na-Gael, 122-124, 126-127, 129, 139

Clem, Johnny, "Drummer Boy of Chickamauga", third insert

Cleveland, Grover, 73

Cleveland, Ohio, 3

Coercion Act, 127

Colfax, Speaker of the House Schuyler, 77

Collins, Michael, 40

Congress, U.S., 54, 56-57, 66, 73, 84, 164

Connaught Province, Ireland, 34

County Mayo, Ireland, 31, 111

Cromwell, Oliver, 4, 15, 29-30, 33-36, 41, 130, 143, 155

Cronin, Dr. Patrick, 124-125, 127-129, 139

Custer, General George Armstrong, 114

Danville Prison, 99

D'Arcy, William, 103

Davenport, First Bishop, 158

Davitt, Michael, 134

Denison, George, 150

Detroit, Michigan, 3, 20, 22, 25, 31, 45, 47- 48, 51, 64, 66, 78, 80, 82, 84, 86-87, 93, 96-97, 114-115, 121, 125-126, 137-139, 164-166

Bob-Lo, playground of Detroit, 115

Bois Blanc, 31

Detroit Free Press, 60

Detroit News, 14

Detroit Tribune, 87-88

Donnelly, Katherine, 48, 87, 90-91

"Dynamitards", 127, 139

Dynamite War, 126, 129, 140

Earl of Antrim, 36

Eastport, Maine, 70

Eccles Hill, Battle at, 102

Edison, Samuel, 32

Edison, Thomas Alva, 13, 19

Elizabethan Conquests, 30, 34

Emmet, Robert, 16

English Civil Wars, 33

Erin's Hope, 18

Executive Mansion, 60, 80

The White House, 60

"Fall of Parnell", 141

Famine, 36, 155

Fenian Brigades, 61

Fenian Brotherhood, 4, 15, 78, 107, 149, 159, 161, 169

Fenianism, 17, 24, 29, 88, 93, 121, 154-156, 158-159, 161

Fenian Proclamation, 37

Fenian "Ram", 152-153

"Fenian Scare", 20, 63

Fenian "War Bonds", 58

Fianna, 15, 149

Ford, Henry, 138-139

Fort Amherstburg, 165

Fort Detroit, 166

Fort Erie, 23, 71, 86, 150

Fort Gratiot, 65

Fort Mackinac, 165

Fort Pembina, 107

Foster, George, United States Marshal, 100-103

Franklin, New York, 100-101, 105-106

Fremont, Elkhorn & Missouri Valley Railroad, 116

French and Indian War, 165

Gable, Clark, 137, 142

Gaelic Language, 15, 34

George V, 144

Gettysburg, Battle of, 24, 72

Gladstone, William E., 88, 121-124, 126, 130-137, 139-141, 143-144

"Glorious Revolution", 131

Grant, President Ulysses S., 95, 101, 106

Great Western railway, 52

Growth of Popery Act, 30

Henry Ford Museum, 139

Henry VIII, 36

Holland, John, 152-153

Holt County, Nebraska, 113, 115

"Home Rule", 122-123, 127, 129-134, 139, 141, 143

Horseshoe Ridge, Battle of, 12

House of Commons, 59, 123, 130-131, 141

House of Lords, 121, 131, 141

Hull, William, 165

Hunley, CSS, 152

"Invasion funds", 51, 80, 157

IRA, 127

Irish Brigade,
    23rd Illinois, 16, 160
    Fighting 69th, 16

Irish Free State, 144

Irish Land League, 122, 126, 130, 134

Irish Nationalist Party, 137

Irish Republican Brotherhood (IRB), 15, 18, 59, 127

Irish Sea, 33

James II, 131

Jefferson, Thomas, 3, 57, 165

Johnson, President Andrew, 23, 53, 56, 59-60, 68, 70, 72, 78-79

Jones' Wood, New York, 62

Kearsarge, USS, 55

Kenrick, Archbishop, 159

Killian, Bernard, 60-61, 70, 78

King, Martin Luther, 29

Knoxville, siege of, 67

Lake Erie, 51, 66, 69, 165, 168

Lake Huron, 49

Lake Shore & Michigan Southern R.R., 3

Lambton County, Ontario, 25, 65, 90

Le Caron, Major Henri (alias Thomas Miller Beach), 79-80, 100, 125, 128
    alias Dr. Morton, 125

Lee, General Robert E., 11, 16

Lewistown, New York, 166

Liberal Unionists, 131

Limerick, Ireland, 25, 31

Lincoln, Abraham, 53, 55, 79

London Bridge bombing, 123

London, England, 23, 56, 72, 77, 121-124, 126, 131, 140

London Times, 140

Longstreet, General James, 12

Louisville, Kentucky, 99

Lynch, General W. F., 69

Lyons, Lida, 13, 138

Mackenzie's Rebellion of 1837, 24, 73

Mackinac Island, 31, 115, 165

Madison, James, 3, 164-166

Malone, New York, 100-102, 106

Manitoba, raid in 1871, 112

McDermott, General John, 82, 95

McDonald, John A., Canada's first
    Prime Minister, 61

McGee, Thomas D'Arcy, "Father of
    Confederation", fourth insert

McMahon, Rev. John, 86

McMicken, Gilbert, Canadian
    Intelligence Chief, 79

McMullen, Archbishop John, 17,
    158-161

    Western Tablet, 160

Meade, General George, 24, 72

Meagher, Thomas, 16, second insert

Michigan, USS, 72, 167, 168, 169

    Bryson, Captain Andrew, 167,
    168

    Kelly, Engineer James P., 169

    Murphy, Pilot Patrick, 168

Militia Act of 1868, 92

Moffat Mansion, New York, 18

Molly Maguires, 37, 155

Monroe, James, 3, 164

Montgomery Guards, 96

Moore, Stephen, Michigan lumber
    baron, 138

Mulligan, Brigadier General James,
    16-17, 159-161

    Fort Mulligan, West Virginia,
    160

    Second Battle of Kernstown, 160

Muskegon, Michigan, 22

Nashville, Tennessee, 68, 79

Nebraska, 5, 31, 81, 107, 111, 113-116

Neutrality Act, 72, 73, 101

Niagara Campaign, 166

Niagara Falls, 166

Niagara Peninsula, 23, 69, 72, 164

Niagara River, 65, 72, 167-168

Navy Island, Ontario, 63

New York Times, 140

Niedhardt, W. S., 93

Non-Intercourse Act, 164

Norman Conquests, 29

Northern Ireland, 124, 143-144

O'Brien, William, Editor of *United Ireland*, 134
O'Brien, Lucy, 24, 38
O'Brien, Sir Edward, 38
O'Brien, Sir Lucius, 38
O'Brien, William Smith, 24, 38, 89
O'Connell, Daniel, 16, 40
O'Donoghue, William, 107
Oglesby, Richard, Illinois Governor, 134
O'Mahony, John, 18, 29, 58-60, 62, 78, 149
O'Neill, General John, 23, 52, 67-73, 77-82, 84, 86, 89, 91-92, 94, 96, 99-103, 105-107, 111-117, 121, 151, 154, 156, 161, 163, 167-169
O'Neill's "second invasion", 154
O'Neill, Nebraska, 111, 114
"Orange card", 131
O'Shea, Captain William Henry, 139
O'Shea, Katherine (Katie), 139

Parliament, British, 33
Parliament, Canadian, 93
Parliament, Irish, 35
Parnell, Charles Stewart, 123, 125-127, 131-132, 134, 137-142
Passamaquoddy Bay, 70
Paterson Museum, New Jersey, 153

Patriot War, 24
Peel, Sir Robert, 121
Penal Laws, 35
Philadelphia, Pennsylvania, 18, 80-82, 84-86, 93, 111, 121
Philadelphia Age, 81-82
"Phoenix Park murders", 123
"Pine belt", 19, 57
Pinkerton Agency, 45-48, 57, 78, 81, 89
Pinkerton, Allan, 46-51, 66, 90, 157
Pingree, Governor Hazen, third insert
"Planters", 30
Port Huron, Michigan, 3, 11, 13, 14, 19-22, 24, 29-32, 45, 47-51, 57, 59, 62, 64-65, 78, 81, 84, 86-87, 90, 93, 96, 105-107
    Customs Inspector, 13
    Fort Gratiot, 65
    Launch point for invasion, 49
    Port Huron High School, 25
    Port Huron Newspapers, 31
    Ward One neighborhood, 13
    Port Huron Press, 11, 20, 56, 62, 63
St. Clair County, 14, 21
St. Clair River, 21, 32, 48-49, 64, 90
Protectorate, The, 34

Queen Elizabeth, 143

Queen's Own, 4, 49, 93

Queenston Heights, Battle of, 166

Queen Victoria, 52

Randall, Samuel, Speaker of the
     House, 134

"Reading law", 87

Reconstruction, 53, 84

Reilly, Father Charles O., 122

Richmond, Quebec, 55, 94, 100

Ridgeway, Battle of, 23, 24, 37, 71, 77,
     79-81

Riel, Louis, 107

Roberts, William, 18, 62, 78, 80

Rome, New York, 97-100

Rosecrans, General William S., 12

Royal Navy, 152-153, 163

Sarnia, Ontario, 23, 32, 49-50, 52,
     62-65, 90, 93

Scapa Flow, 152, 153

Scotland Yard, 79, 122

Semmes, Captain Raphael,
     first insert

Seward, Secretary of State William,
     60-61

Sherman, General William
     Tecumseh, 11

Shiloh Campaign, 151

Slavery, Catholic Irish, 29, 33, 40

St. Ambrose College, 158

St. Albans, Vermont, 56, 99-100

St. Jean, Quebec, 94, 100

St. Lawrence Seaway, 52, 94

St. Louis Republican, 159

St. Mary's Seminary in Baltimore,
     126

St. Paul, Minnesota, 158

Stanton, Secretary of War, 60

Stephens, James, first insert

Sullivan, Alexander, 125-127, 129,
     134

Sumner, Senator Charles, 56

Supreme Tribunal in Rome, 154

Sweeny, General "Fighting Tom", 65,
     69, 72, 78, 94, 151, 163

Tasmania, 39

Tecumseh, Shawnee leader, 165

Thomas, General George H.,
     third insert

"Thousand mile front", 65, 151

Toledo, Ohio, 3

Tories, 132, 134

Toronto, Ontario, 24-25, 32, 71-73,
     86, 105, 167

Tower of London bombing, 123

Ulster, Protestant Northern Ireland, 30, 46, 98, 143

Ulster Unionist Party, 143

United States Navy, 153

University of Michigan Law School, 21, 125

University of Michigan Medical School, 125

Van Rensselaer, Major General Stephen, 166

Vatican, 36, 155-156

Verdon, Lawrence, 20

War Between The States (Civil War), 4, 11-12, 16-19, 21-22, 32, 37, 54-55, 61, 67, 85, 87, 89, 95-96, 150, 158, 160

War Department, U.S., 49-50

War of 1812, 24, 55, 163, 165

Warwick, Ontario, 32

Welles, Gideon, Secretary of the Navy, 60, 169

West Indies, 33

"White City" murders, 128

Whitehall Gardens, 121

William III of Orange-Nassau, 131

Windsor, Ontario, 52, 66, 93

Young Ireland Revolt of 1848, 16, 39

About the Author

Michael Plemmons began his career as a sports writer and Associated Press features contributor on the Gulf Coast. He has since worked in Washington, Milwaukee, Chicago and Tokyo, writing on subjects from professional football, crime and government to architecture and the arts. His work has appeared in dozens of periodicals, and his short stories in a number of acclaimed fiction anthologies and textbooks.

Michael studied under Howard Mahan at the University of South Alabama, where he earned a history baccalaureate with honors, and with biographer John Bartlow Martin at Northwestern University (Master's program).

He now lives in Wisconsin.

CPSIA information can be obtained at www.ICGtesting.com
Printed in the USA
236869LV00001B/107/P